STAY A FRIEND
as Long as You Can

STAY A FRIEND
as Long as You Can

A Memoir

Virginia Weir

for Robert

STAY A FRIEND AS LONG AS YOU CAN

PART I

PART II

No One is Named Marvin Anymore

Quite a Day

A Pile of Peanuts and a Prayer Garden

Easter After Easter

A Last Speech

Hopes and Shoulds

Eighty

No More Pruning

An Afternoon in the Bronx

Fucking Narcissists

Mattapoisett

Slippages

Bad Directions

I Get the Job Done

NAMI

A Little Late

In the Foxhole, 2017

Mission Critical

"The Joy of a Day"

And in the days
when you find yourself orphaned,
emptied
of all wind-singing, of light,
the pieces of cursed bread on your tongue,

may there come back to you
a voice,
spectral, calling you
sister!
from everything that dies.

And then
you shall open
this book, even if it is the book of nightmares.

Galway Kinnell

from "Under the Maud Moon"
The Book of Nightmares

Part I

Rescue
2004

I didn't want to be scared to enter his apartment, but I was, a little. What dark night of his soul would be revealed? The window over the kitchen sink looked out on a breezeway, a black plastic bag draped awkwardly over the blinds so that They couldn't see in. Tall shutter doors formed a makeshift division between the bed and the small main room. The smell of mold caught in my throat. How long had it been since he slept on the stripped bed, piled up with clothes and newspapers?

It was early evening, not particularly cold in San Francisco even for January, but Robert had been there on the curb in his heavy winter jacket and knit cap waiting for me as I pulled up in the rental car. He looked stern, old, ragged. His jacket was dirty. I got out of the car and we hugged each other, one of his long, hard hugs. I did not ask how he was.

"It's been impossible," he had said, abruptly. "I haven't slept here in days. I have been staying with Doreen, from the bookstore."

I had never been to this apartment, where Robert had settled after we sold the house on De Haro Street and John and I moved to the east coast. It was odd to think he had lived for

12 years now in this average, pale yellow, stucco building on 6th Avenue near the park, pinned between other similar buildings, with a door by the garage and two upper floors. Robert pulled an enormous, noisy bangle of keys from his pocket, unlocked the door by the garage, and we passed through a long concrete hallway to his apartment at the back. One dim overhead bulb shone an eerie green over the brown bags lining the hall, packed tight with newspapers.

"It may not look like it, but I have been trying to pack everything up," he said. "I couldn't work at night, though. They're always around."

We went two steps down, into another small hall. Except for the kitchenette, everything was carpeted, even the bathroom. The landlord had decorated the living room wall with mirror squares as if to make the room seem larger. Windows at the back of the room revealed a patio and small ground-level garden. For an almost-basement apartment, there was a fair amount of light.

It was not unlivable, except for the piles of newspapers and crushed plastic bags everywhere, a foot deep in some areas. Beyond that, boxes. Those familiar, ever-present boxes of books that he moved from place to place over the last 30 years, never unpacking them: three rows deep, four rows wide, five boxes high. More newspapers, rolled-up bath rugs, and other miscellaneous items were piled on top of the boxes.

Robert showed me around as though this was a normal living situation, pointing out seven tightly taped boxes of items he definitely wanted to ship to the east coast. The rest were to be decided upon.

"I got rid of the truck," he reminded me. "A couple guys came and got it last week."

"That's good." I had learned how to drive standard in that truck, a magnificent 1968 yellow Ford with a shell on the back, used many times to move me and other family members and friends from apartment to apartment. Lately, he said, he had been moving the truck from side to side of the block in sync with the city street cleaners. Occasionally he let a homeless couple sleep in the back. When the voices got too bad in his apartment, he slept in the cab. I think he believed that if things got impossible he would be able to leave the city and live from his truck, but it had been breaking down more often and would not last long.

I was tired after the six-hour flight, and we had our work cut out for us the next day. "Let's go eat," I said. At a Vietnamese restaurant just around the corner, I ordered noodles and Robert had a bowl of soup. I kept a light conversation going, talking about my children—Kevin, who was in college in Boston, and Clara in middle school—and my fundraising job at a family service agency back in Connecticut.

Robert listened intently. He hadn't removed his jacket and his pockets were so stuffed, both inside and outside, that at first glance he looked obese. "What's in your pockets?" I asked.

"All my papers, anything important." He shrugged. "I can't leave anything in the apartment." I looked at him straight on for the first time since I arrived. I had been too afraid to until now. Now almost 71, skinny and pale but still handsome, his thin hair was a brilliant white, the white beard carefully trimmed around the same full lips.

He paid cash for dinner. I was staying with a friend who, in a strange coincidence, lived just around the corner. Robert would stay with his co-worker from the bookstore again. I walked him to the streetcar and we stood there quietly on the corner for a few minutes waiting for the next train. The misty January air made the rails shine. Fog billowed overhead, threatening to dip down and envelope us. I missed this city.

Finally, he smiled at me. "I'm glad you're here."

December 1994

Dear Robert,

Here's hoping Secret Service aren't reading this letter. But if they are, well, I hope they enjoy it.

I say that about three-quarters tongue-in-cheek. The other quarter is reserved for the possibility that they really are reading it. We didn't hear from you about all that, and maybe it really was a bout of paranoia. I alternated back and forth during the phone conversation, wondering. On the one hand, it was ridiculous; on the other, if I were a federal investigator, your entire life would be suspicious to me.

There's a title for you: "Your Entire Life Would Be Suspicious"....

V

It was in the fall of 1994, ten years earlier, when Robert first called to tell me and my husband John that he felt quite sure he was being followed. There was a team of them, he said, mostly men but an occasional woman, who would trail him when he

4

would walk to the local café to have coffee, who would say something to him as they brushed by him on the street. He was beginning to recognize some of them. This had been going on for a few months when he called.

"But why?" we asked. "Why would they follow you?"

He had been gambling, he said. I knew he had supported himself occasionally by betting—on greyhounds, horses, the stock market. Who knows how often he did it, or why, or how much money he made. He had mentioned at least one bad time when he lost a lot.

Robert liked speculation, considering an allotment of factors and situations and imagining the outcome. He did this careful considering about everything in his life, to the point where sometimes he couldn't make a move, could not do anything at all.

He told us that earlier in the year he had won at the racetrack and used a hundred-dollar bill from that win to place another bet. Authorities had pulled him aside, taken him to an upstairs room at the track and interrogated him. They said the bill was counterfeit. Robert protested that he had gotten the bill there at the track, that he knew nothing else.

Shortly after that, he said, the surveillance began.

"I just wanted you to know." His tone on the phone had been very somber. The idea of him being followed was frightening, but not impossible. He did live an isolated, eccentric life; in its predictable dailiness he could fit the profile of a Unabomber; he could be someone who was of interest to the government, we supposed. But what were we to do, and at this distance?

The next call came a few months later. This time Robert sounded more indignant and more desperate. They had moved in upstairs and were keeping track of everything he did. At night They were bringing people into the flat upstairs and trying to get them to identify him and testify against him. He was beginning to think he needed a lawyer, but he couldn't afford one. We talked a long time. Having lived across the country from him for the past six years, John and I waffled back and forth about what we believed was actually happening, but we didn't tell Robert that. There was something in his voice—his calmness, that familiar authority—that kept us from prodding. In many ways it was easier to believe that the Feds were following and videotaping him than to wonder what it meant that he was imagining these things, and what to do about it.

We called a lawyer friend who lived in San Francisco, who agreed to see Robert and discuss the situation.

After the appointment, our friend called us. "He's loony," he said. "It's all in his head." I had expected that was what he would conclude, but the casualness of his remark stung me.

There were no further phone calls from Robert for a while after that. None of us wanted to talk about what was not happening, or his belief that it was.

I wrote to him regularly. I hoped what I thought was his paranoia would ease up. When I saw him on my occasional visits to the Bay Area over the next several years, we didn't speak of it. In March 2003, Robert sent a disturbing letter:

> ...The Feds have been hounding me <u>seriously</u> and
> very heavy handedly... They moved in above me in

October and watch me every moment at home. They are recording everything, so I do not answer the phone or call out. They follow me everywhere; each day to work and back, to the grocery store, coffee shop, etc... Because they can hear me all the time at home, I've told them to go to hell and worse more than once. They are persistent and adamant and do not seem to have any intention to leave in the near future.

They took a "psychological" profile by interrupting my sleep; an expert with some sophisticated electronic gear was the agent for this. Needless to say, it is remarkable that the Feds now think they have carte blanc *legally and can do whatever they want since Sept. 11*[th]*. Obviously they will not disclose what the hell they're up to without strong legal pressure by experienced federal lawyers. Who the hell can afford that?*

I phoned the ACLU—they asked me if this was related to Sept. 11th*. I said I have no idea; they did not seem to be interested in pursuing the matter.*

I will try legal aid next, but I am very doubtful they will be able to help.

All of this takes a toll, and time. And time is all I really have right now so I really resent they're taking it from me. What I have is my own resolve. And the knowledge that I've done nothing wrong.

Moreover, they must already know that I have done nothing at all; that I'm "small" in any scheme of things; so why are they still here? When stupidity and its consequences contrive with the Government, people mean nothing at all.

So, I have not written because they watch my mail, and I don't want anyone involved in this, especially

not you or John and the family... This is very serious:
stay out of it, you can rely on their ruthless disregard
of rights or privacy or anything else. And I am quite...

The last page of the letter was missing. It was obvious things were slipping for him.

John and I implored him to take a vacation, to come east, and in the fall of 2003 he finally did, extending his visit from two weeks to a month. In the nine years since that first phone call, Robert had grown tired and worn down by the persecution he felt. Every day on his visit with us in Connecticut he went on a long walk. We went to church together. We ate a lot, drank wine, watched movies.

It had been years, he said, since he had been to a movie.

October 2003

After a few days with him here, I feel some of the old responses, my sense of his expectations of me— that I would be a Writer and Reader (that I would read and write "better" than I do)... that I would push myself in ways that I haven't... that I would "turn out" in ways that I haven't. I remember now. I hated being pushed by someone who continually turned his back on all opportunities... for love, for money.... and now we are both older. He is old. And there's a sense of ellipses everywhere... lost time, just loss everywhere, an unraveling.... he and I experience the world in a very similar way; we always have. I don't mind living in loss; it is all loss. But I can't let it into the center of myself.

During his visit, we didn't talk about the people following him, or the voices he heard. He went back to San Francisco reluctantly, but resolved. Resolution was not enough.

Dec. 21 03

Dear Virginia,

This has been a horrendous week... But today the sun has come out, and I've come to the Arboretum in Golden Gate Park... and these days I feel very grateful to be here.

This is what is happening right now: the 'head' or coordinator of this investigation has been talking to people who know me, and is now convinced that I am not the person they are looking for; that they have been mistaken from the beginning and intends to close the intense "monitoring" they've been giving me no later than Monday. He may have gone to Washington to explain this and get approval for the shutdown. All this I have heard in the last 4 days via the hardwood floor acoustics after I've been awakened by another attempt to get someone to testify against me. Each night I pray for God's intervention since He knows I'm innocent in this matter, but it is not so easy for me. Each night I hear the two agents urging someone to claim that I worked with him on some criminal act: "Just say the word and I'll run him downtown" etc. And this frightens me so much that I cannot sleep. They have put a high intensity white light above my bed which makes everything visible to them, and so when the voice warns me, I put black things over my head and the quilt and a pillow and bury my face in the mattress. But the light is so bright, it's as if I'm lying in an intense white field of light. But my face is down, so the person they bring in cannot see it, and cannot say yes that's the guy.

...I was so frightened this morning that I thought of phoning you and John and telling you they were going to arrest me— and now again, God intervenes and the guy backs off.

This is like my own tiny Iraq, threatened constantly by people trying to harm me. The agents don't give a damn about whether I actually did something criminal, they simply want to throw me in jail. Some 'unbiased' investigation!

But, God willing, this will be the last of it, and by Christmas Eve they will be gone. So this is my "ambivalence." I believe, truly, that God has intervened and protected me, and I thank God and Jesus, and Mary, and the saints for their extraordinary help and yet I am still quite frightened and worried that on even this supposed last day something will change their minds.

... So I will go home and go directly to bed. I will try to sleep in my boxed-in cubby hole, a small area with boxes around and above me that I've shaped. It is too small and I can't stretch out and it hurts my knees, but I feel much safer, since I cannot be seen even in their dreadful light, which doesn't quite cover the area.

I have nowhere else to go. It is not easy to be alone with all this; there is no one here I can ask to put me up, and there is certainly no one like you and John to help me out.

It is the weight of it and its constancy and the terrible threat that it contains that strangles my heart and mind. So if it will end this week, one of the things

I have to avoid is the aloneness and separation I chose for far too long...

I wish you the happiest Christmas, for you and John and Kevin and Clara to whom I owe so much.

Love, Robert

The delusions were terrible enough that he was calling us at least once a week. On one call just after Christmas he wept, sick with a bad case of bronchitis from sleeping on the concrete floor of the hallway, the only place They weren't monitoring him.

I talked to a psychiatrist at work about him. "Sounds like delusional disorder," he said calmly, impressed that Robert had been able to keep his job as a clerk in a bookstore for the past few years. "Don't bother to try and convince him that 'they' aren't real. He won't believe you, and he may even think you're against him."

I looked up "Delusional Disorder" in the diagnostic manual: formerly called "paranoid disorder," considered a serious mental illness, where a person cannot tell what is real from what is imagined. The delusions are not supernatural, though; they involve situations that could occur in real life, such as being followed, deceived, conspired against, or loved from a distance. They usually involve the misinterpretation of perceptions or experiences. Robert's disorder sounded like it was of the "persecutory" type.

I took a long walk. Why couldn't he just leave the city and come out here, I wondered. He could stay with us until he found a job and a place. He could start over. Perhaps, living near us, the voices would go away. Absorbed in the potential happiness of that, I didn't think more.

"What do you think?" I asked John, over dinner.

"Yes," he said immediately, "Ask him." John didn't say then what was on his mind, that if I didn't go out there and get him, Robert would likely go down, rather quickly, in a hospital first for his physical and then for his mental condition. Then, perhaps, homelessness. And then, and then. He probably wouldn't last long.

We thought of Robert's visit in the fall, the way we could see him unfolding, happiness rising in his face. So I called him and said, "Move east, stay with us for a while. What's there in the city to keep you now?" He agreed without hesitation. Within a week he had quit his job. I offered to come and help him pack up on my annual visit to my family, and I bought him a one-way ticket to fly home with me.

I met him at the apartment the next morning with coffee for us both and a box of plastic lawn bags. He was wearing the same clothes as the day before, looking just as tired. The mess of his place seemed more daunting in the daylight, the mirrored wall amplifying the chaos. I am not going to think about this, I said to myself. Not think, just do.

"We're going to have to toss ruthlessly," I said aloud, cheerfully. "You're not going to be angry, are you, as we go through all this stuff?" I had put on my administrative role, and I would live in that role for the day. We were not going to speak of what was obvious—that he had fallen apart.

"No, do it," Robert said.

"Okay. Why don't you start at your desk? You're the only one who knows which papers to keep and which to toss."

Robert's "desk" was our old coffee tabletop, made of laminated teak floor squares on particle board, held up by three boxes on one side and the windowsill on the other. There were other small evidences of my past life, too—things that John and I had left behind from the house we had all lived in together: the dresser and nightstand from Goodwill, a couple of rolled-up posters that had been on our living room wall, a Mexican blanket we used to drape over the couch, the old radio-tape player—a gift for John's 28th birthday. It was jarring to see these objects, so three-dimensional, completely strange in their familiarity.

"Put the radio on," I said, "I like music when I work."

We worked around the corner from each other in the dark apartment with the radio playing NPR, with news on the hour. There was so much to do. Focus, I told myself; keep it simple. Don't let yourself get overwhelmed, just move forward steadily. Occasionally I glanced over my shoulder to see what Robert was doing, momentarily disarmed by our reflections in the mirror wall. It was hard to look at him, so thin and old, practically a stranger. I looked steady and solid, like a mom. *Well, that's what I am*, I thought. *I'm a mom. I'm a caretaker and caregiver. I'm a fixer.* I couldn't tell if Robert was making any headway on the pile of envelopes on the desk, and I decided not to pay attention. Perhaps he just needed to sit.

I began in the bedroom. The closet contents were strange. Everything had been dry cleaned, from the nicest slacks (I counted about 20 pairs, hardly worn) to threadbare shirts, ripped sweatshirts, and old neckties full of holes. There were a lot of sweaters (although I had rarely seen him wear any) with a tendency toward stripes, and a multitude of red shirts. At the beginning I asked Robert what he thought about keeping this or that, but after a while I stopped asking. We would never finish if we deliberated. On the bed: a pile of clothes to ship; in the center of the room, a bag to toss. Another for Goodwill, labeled "Men's Clothes". Each time I filled up two lawn bags, I took them out to the hallway.

Then I went through the dresser drawers, filled with muscle supports—knee wraps, wrist wraps, ankle wraps—and tiny running shorts. For many years Robert ran several miles a day. How could I have forgotten that? There were perhaps 30 pairs of new socks, still in the bag. And here were six pairs of women's thong underwear, size 6, new with tags. I held them up to him, trying to make a joke: "I'm not even going to ask." Robert shrugged solemnly and said he had no idea. Whose underwear could they have been? Could he have bought them? Could they have been Diane's?

Knee-deep in dry cleaning plastic wrap and hangers, with an old red sweatshirt (thoroughly clean) in one hand and the thong underwear in the other, I said, suddenly, "Robert, do you know... this... cleaning up... is what people do when someone has died. This is what they do!" We looked at each other across the room for a long moment. "So. I'm glad you're alive."

I felt suddenly hopeful. There was a chance here. I laughed. A pause, and then he laughed, that big, wild, rare laugh of his. "Me, too!"

His inability to categorize or organize his own things in any way was apparent and startling. Throughout the day he had found several hundred dollars in various folded envelopes, among old bank statements, in two half-filled metal file boxes. It was like he tried to organize, left it, and started over again at another time, with a new box, new supplies.

He told me later that I had accidentally thrown out some cash that was stashed in an old box of frozen waffles in the freezer.

Had he always been this way? I wondered. Had I mistaken disability for eccentricity all these years?

In the kitchenette he rummaged through the drawers, and then I followed discreetly to toss their contents. There were large bags of walnuts in the cabinets, some good and some rancid. (Everything Robert liked he bought in quantity.) He wanted to keep the pans and some of the silverware. "They're good pans," he said—very serious and tense and tired—but they weren't.

I put them aside for consideration.

Everywhere: envelopes and plastic bags tucked here and there, some wrapped in rubber bands. Stacks of unused paper towels, carefully folded into small squares. Was this hoarding new? It wasn't a habit I remembered from before, but after Robert moved to the city I was rarely in his apartments. Like a nesting bird he had collected piles of toothpicks and small stacks of the colored plastic tabs from bread bags—on the table, on the counter, on the dresser, on top of the newspaper piles—everywhere.

Also, throughout the apartment I found envelopes addressed to him in my handwriting, letters and packages of poems, journals, and photos I had sent him over the past 30 years and before. Seeing all these envelopes startled me; how earnest I was, how optimistic to have continued writing to him all these years. And even though he rarely responded to my letters, he had kept me near him.

Coming closer, pulling away, that is what we did. So often, like that apartment wall, I was alone in a room of mirrors when I was with Robert. I laid out a story to him, my story, over and over again. I was talking to myself while he watched and felt whatever he felt and could not or would not articulate. I had said all this to him—that so much of us was all about me, that the lack of him was an imbalance, a heavy weight between us. He acknowledged this was true. "There was no place for it to go," he said, meaning his longing and his losses—his cultivated loneliness, like a can of compressed air. And the guilt of all he wasn't for everyone who was for him—that weight.

The next largest task was the boxes, which took up over half of the small living room. I suggested we open them all and sort through them quickly.

"Why bother?" he said. "Just toss them. Why open them up and have to make more decisions?"

But I could tell he was sad about throwing out good books, so before the afternoon was over we sliced open all the boxes. The ones on the bottom were moldy, stuck to the damp carpeting, and they fell apart when I tried to pick them up. All those years I had watched him move the books from place to place, so carefully boxed (even that day he bragged about the durability of the double-cardboard), never unpacked. The books had become precious, secret, emblematic of all I didn't know about him.

As I went through the boxes with him, I was startled, again. Although he had every book by some authors (Kundera, Merwin, Kazanzakis…) they were mostly paperback, not in great shape: replaceable.

"That's a first edition," he said of a philosophy book. "You can't get it anymore; it's out of print."

Of what use was the book to him? Of what use was it ever to him? (I didn't mention the availability of books on the internet.)

"Well, keep it if you want." He held it a moment, then put it in the box to toss.

Every couple of hours I took a break, hiking up the block to the parking lot to feed the meter for my rental car from a huge can of old quarters that Robert conveniently found. It was a relief to be forced out into the sunny west coast air, so familiar, such a contrast to the cave of his apartment.

When I came back this time I said, "I've got an idea. Let's not toss these books. This is the city—someone will want them. Let's put the books out on the sidewalk over the weekend. I bet people will take them."

Robert seemed amenable to this idea. I made a few signs: FREE BOOKS.

My sister called to check on me and gave me the name of a hauler she had used before to pick up junk. I made arrangements for Robert to stay at my brother's, since he couldn't stay at his co-worker's house that night.

Toward evening, from the apartment upstairs, I heard the sounds of a chair being pushed back, water running, and muffled talking, like a family having dinner. How could he really believe that there were "investigators" up there?

We fed the parking meter again and ate a sandwich and salad for dinner at a restaurant around the corner, discussing what was next. "I'll figure out a place to stay this week," he said, "do what needs to be done, and fly home with you next week." He asked me to write a list of the things he needed to cancel, and the things to tell the hauler to pick up. Writing this list made both of us feel better.

"You know, when you come back with us, we're not going to be polite anymore," I said. "We won't let you do your disappearing act anymore. We'll hassle you. But you're used to that now, right?"

I was trying to get him to smile, but he wouldn't. "Here," Robert said, rummaging in the inner pockets of his coat. He handed me a thick folded envelope bound with a rubber band and wrapped in a clear plastic bag. "It's very possible," he said in a low tone, frowning, "that they might not let me get on the plane when we go. I simply don't know. Take this cash and keep it for me."

I pictured federal agents surrounding us at the airport, ordering us to put our hands up. Looking at his sad, contained face, part of me longed to be arrested. I could laugh, "It's true! It's true!" and in being caught we'd all be free.

Later I counted $1,700 in small bills.

An appointment was made for a hauler to dispose of 60 lawn bags of trash, two battered dressers, a bed frame and mattress. Although there was still plenty to do, we had made major progress; Robert would work on it over the next several days. He called someone to clean the apartment. Later in the week I would spend another day with him to finish. Then on Saturday morning, I would be back to pick him up to go to the airport. That was the plan.

"It's my birthday, you know," I said after we taped and labeled the last box.

"I know."

"Well, let's have a drink!" I drove us across the city in the rental car to the touristy Cliff House and we found a table by the window overlooking the ocean. A plate of fruit and cheese and bottle of wine softened the long day.

"Remember that first birthday of mine, at the diner in Fort Collins?"

"Of course."

"Well," I said, trying to lift us up, "Happy birthday to me," and he laughed. The sun went down one red eighth-inch at a time through the big plate glass window.

It was gray and foggy in San Francisco on the Saturday I picked Robert up to fly back with me to Connecticut. He was waiting on the corner of Dolores Street, outside his co-worker's apartment where he had been staying at night, sleeping very little. Mid-week I had borrowed my brother-in-law's truck and come down to the city again. We had packed up all the boxes of books and clothes and papers he was keeping and shipped them to the east coast.

On the way to the airport via 19th Avenue, past San Francisco State University and other familiar landmarks of my earlier life, merging onto 280 and then 380 and then 101, I made small talk about the weather, the extra suitcase I had bought for him, about returning the rental car. Something about the week had made us efficient; we checked in the maximum number of bags, bought sandwiches for the long flight, acted casual in the waiting area by the gate. There was an odd normalcy about the day, as though this were any situation, any trip, as though we'd done it many times before.

Soon we were on the plane, rising over the East Bay toward the mountains. No one had come to arrest him; no one had come except me.

"Maybe the voices… maybe it's God talking to me," Robert said. "Maybe the voices were there so that I would have to change my life."

"Maybe." I took his hand.

"I'm very lucky."

"Yes, you are."

"Thank you."

I held his hand and looked out the plane window at the rolling winter-green hills, growing smaller. Everything seemed new and possible again. He was safe. We were together. I felt alive, exuberant—outside time, almost. I felt his gratitude as my own.

Like a Lover
1975

The story of Robert is the story of me, too. I can't get around or away from that. We're together like… like what? Father and daughter, yes. Teacher and student. Lovers who never made love—and thank god for that.

The first time we talked was my seventeenth birthday, at the diner across from the Colorado State University campus where I was a new freshman and Robert taught Introduction to

Philosophy. I had boldly invited him to go out for tea, leaving a note on his office door. We talked (I talked) for five hours. I remember that I ate an open-faced turkey sandwich with gravy, which he paid for, and I was grateful because I had no money.

What did we talk about those five hours? I hardly recall. I found out he was unmarried and had no children. Then I simply told him everything, everything I could think of about my 17 years—my family, my fast-food job before college, writing poetry. I described my other classes, who was teaching them, and what it felt like to be in college for two weeks.

I was bold, and there I sat, having dinner with a college professor! It was as though everything was before me, my whole life. I was 200 miles from home; it was January and I had entered college mid-year; I didn't know anyone. I hated the high school I had attended in Pueblo, and with some maneuvering had arranged to graduate a year early. But we hadn't made any arrangements for college. That fall my father took me on a one-day, three-college tour in northern Colorado: Greeley, Colorado State, and the University of Colorado. From the hour we spent in Fort Collins, Colorado State, seemed like a place I would be able to navigate. It was an "aggie" school known for its veterinary college. We didn't even get out of the car in Greeley (which at that time looked like a big farm to me) or Boulder (which, with its crowds of long-haired men and women with fashionable hiking boots, seemed like too much of a party school). Decision made, we drove the three hours back to Pueblo that same day.

For six months I worked fulltime at Arby's, fought off the lecherous manager, and saved my money. How mature and careful and naïve I was! The month before I left home I asked an older friend of mine if he would have sex with me so that at least I wouldn't be afraid of it when I arrived at college. I felt scared and free. This feeling of anticipation, of possibility, was there the first time Robert and I talked and in most of the hundreds of other five-hour talks we had over the next decade.

When I met him, Robert was 42, of medium height, with dark brown hair and a barrel chest. This was before he quit smoking and began running. He had a beard, full lips and pensive green eyes. He wore jeans all the time with a thick brown belt and button-down shirt, usually a dark plaid of some sort, and a pullover sweater vest. His heavy hiking boots were the only shoes I ever saw him in. His voice was soft and calm, authoritative. How very casually he would sit on the edge of the desk at the front of the room and observe the class. "Far out," he said, term-of-the-day, when one of us said something interesting. This definitely wasn't high school, but I was skeptical even through my excitement.

I remember the first day in his class quite clearly. I wore jeans and a long-sleeved ribbed shirt, the one with the wide, bright stripes—my favorite. I was aware of myself and knew that the shirt alone would call attention to me. But I didn't talk much in the class. As part of my new college persona, I was hoping to hide my earnestness beneath a casualness I mostly did not feel.

I saw him, and he saw me.

After two weeks in my preferred seat at the back of his class, between jottings on Descartes, Dostoevsky, and Nietzsche, I started writing Robert notes in the spiral class notebook in different colors: red, blue, felt-tip green.

> You are interesting, Mr. Bullshit. I wonder how much
> of your <u>bullshit</u> is bullshit. ... There is something that
> I distrust in you... I once knew a college teacher, a
> "poet", who seemed to be like you and he went to
> bed with many of his students... Seems like both the
> trust and the distrust can fuck you up...

Just two months later, 24 classes and another evening out with him, I wrote a passionate, practically religious poem in that notebook. For 17, it was not a bad poem, and I seemed to know already the roles we were immersed in. The first stanza began:

> O My Father
> you leave me your world
> to step down into naked and new,
> A burning-cold stream

followed by a second:

> O My Teacher
> Your eyes are still and watching
> while mine leap into every flame
> crackling, scorching.

And the romantic finale:

> O My Lover
> Perhaps we will touch but
> Only as the time allows us;
> Then will we slip
> Like summer into fall,
> Four green eyes

We will be,
Still and watching,
The forest and the sea

My eyes are green, like his.

I have kept everything, of course, and over 40 years later, I am embarrassed by these notes. There is something lonely and raw and frightening and impossible in them. I was all spread out with being on my own, trying to create a self.

It was late when Robert and I finally left the diner that first time. We crossed the oval-shaped roundabout on campus, encircled then with gorgeous old Dutch elms. It was cold; we could see our breaths. In the middle of the Oval, quite naturally, we moved toward each other and kissed—long, full, intense—a kiss unlike any of the boys I had known—unsculpted, unanticipated, like stepping into a tide. I pulled back, dizzy almost, disoriented. What did I say then, in all the wisdom of my 17 years? Probably something like, "I don't think I can do this." Even then, I knew an abyss when I was hanging over it.

And what did Robert say? If he said anything, it was simple. "Yes," perhaps. To mean, that he understood. Perhaps he, too, was relieved.

And so our long relationship began.

I never again kissed him on the mouth. In spite of flirting with him and romantic talk in my journals, after that first kiss I did not think about him sexually. It wasn't that I tried not to; I simply didn't. I believed he was trustworthy. That would be the blessed invisible boundary, such as should be with fathers and daughters, or teachers and students. Even later, I did not touch Robert often, not as often as other friends. His hugs were long and concentrated and seemed to require interpretation. There was no room to hug back.

Young as I was, I did not miss the connection between Dostoevsky's *Notes From Underground*, the first book we read in Robert's class, and his home life. Most of the time I knew him he lived in basements, or partially underground. In Fort Collins he rented a basement apartment six or seven blocks from campus. He had no phone. I knew if he was home by whether or not the yellow truck was parked outside.

"So, you're the Underground Man, then," I teased him during one of my first visits to his apartment.

He chuckled and shrugged.

His apartment was tidy and clean but packed as though he might be moving any day and have to leave in a hurry. The front door led into a dark kitchen with a concrete floor, and a bathroom off the side. We never sat in that kitchen; I don't remember a table or chairs or any place to sit. It was an underground world without furniture. There were the boxes of books stacked neatly against the kitchen wall, and some in the tiny front room with a lamp and cushions on the floor where we talked for hours. More boxes functioned as furniture: a table for the toaster, a nightstand for books. In the further room was a mattress on the floor, tightly made with a red blanket.

Occasionally during these talks I would suddenly become exhausted and take a short nap on the bed while Robert read in the other room. The radio was on all the time, volume tuned low on the classical station. He had Coca-Cola to drink and I would help myself to peanut butter on toast until it was late and he walked me back to the dorm.

Sometimes I borrowed a bike, rode to his place, and left a note suggesting we get together, then later we'd meet at the café across from the dorm for coffee and cinnamon rolls. I did all the talking: about classes, my roommate, my new boyfriend from the dorm. (When that boyfriend broke up with me I went straight to Robert's place, but his truck was gone. I waited for a while, crying. I had no paper or pencil, so I scrawled my name in mud, dramatically, on his doorframe. Later that evening he arrived at my dorm room to take me for coffee and let me tell him the story of the boyfriend's betrayal.)

We went to events on campus together—films, concerts, poetry readings—and I felt myself watched by others, as a student with a teacher. He was handsome; I felt intelligent and mysterious with him, and I liked that. I think he did, too.

Of course, our long conversations then were like some kind of making love, some kind of heady imbalance in which I talked, but we didn't talk about him. When I asked questions about him, Robert would answer briefly or shrug and steer the conversation back to me. He had mentioned a former wife, back-when, but did not say much else. In my 17-year-old way I did know he was in love with me, but it remained unspoken, not something he would ever press, and so I could talk and talk and explore myself thoroughly. I felt romantic and safe. This wasn't fair, but I didn't really understand that. It was not as strict as a set of rules—more like a frame I had put on our relationship, and for him to express how he felt about me was on the outside of that frame. Perhaps the talk saved us. I talked us around and around and through our inappropriateness, our dangerous situation, and made an island of safety and trust for myself and probably for him, too.

At the end of my first quarter at college, like a confession, I gave my class notebook to him to read. Robert wrote back a few notes in the margin, red asterisks by some phrases, others underlined. Near the end of the notebook, he had written on a blank page:

> *Last night, a visitor with long black hair. A kiss, short, but flowing as though natural for us. "Wait!"*
> *Had she stayed I would have told her I didn't want to. I wish she would have at least kept me company while I lay awake the rest of the night. Except for a red mark near my collarbone and the strange hot rush of blood that disturbs me even now—I would've thought it was a dream.*

Sometimes I didn't understand what he wrote, and it made me nervous. Was this a dream? A hallucination? Was Robert thinking of me? My hair was long and reddish brown. I didn't believe there was any woman with long black hair visiting him.

There is a rare photo that a friend of mine took of us in that time, standing in front of a tree. It was a hot day in Greeley, Colorado. I wore a T-shirt and jean cut-offs, and my hair was in two braids pinned on top of my head. My legs are long and graceful, 18-year-old legs. He is dark-haired and lanky beside me, in patched jeans and a denim shirt with the sleeves rolled up high. He has his arm around my hip, and mine around his. Not tight. We stand there like we know each other.

In a deep way we did know each other, but in many other ways we didn't. Or, I did not know him. We had been mysterious with each other, gradually assuming we knew each other's feelings, like a secret language where I pretended to understand the code, not wanting to say, *I don't know what you're talking about*, and many times I did not. I acted like I knew how he felt, but I didn't know, and he didn't tell me, not really. Because we both somehow knew if he told me how he felt it might break the frame we had set up and then we might not have a friendship anymore. I think I understood this.

Tucked at the back of the notebook was a slip of recycled mimeograph paper:

If you wrote something for me, you don't have to take the final. If you didn't write anything, you still don't have to take the final. I hope I'll see you before you go. If not, your face and your sound and your touch stay with me.

His special permission both pleased and scared me. I took the final exam.

At the end of the summer of that first fast year of college in 1975, Robert drove me the 200 miles down to Pueblo in his yellow truck. Since my parents' divorce, my sisters and my mother were living in a cracker-box apartment building not far from the house that had just been sold. I hadn't seen them since February. I brought Robert in to meet them, and he and I sat alongside each other on the familiar couch now transplanted to this sad, cramped living room.

"Would you like something to eat, Robert?" my mother asked.

"No, thank you."

"How about something to drink? Iced tea? A Coke?"

"I would have a glass of water if possible. I have to get back to the university today."

"That's a long drive for one day," my mother said. She put some ice and water in a glass and sat down in the chair across from us.

"So, when did classes end, Ginger?" she asked.

"Summer quarter finished Monday," I said. "There's only a couple of weeks before it starts up again."

"Well, that's good! It's a little tight around here," she said. I would be sleeping on the couch the next couple of weeks.

I could see Robert impassively taking in the small rectangle of the living room: couch, TV, end tables, two chairs, brown shag carpeting. The cheap ceiling sparkled.

"So, Robert, how long have you been at Fort Collins?" she asked.

"Eight years."

"And you teach… philosophy?"

"Yes." He wasn't giving her anything extra.

"And so how did Ginger do in your class?"

"She's an excellent student."

He was not going to say anything to invite my mother into a conversation where she could have had a presence. I suddenly felt the awkwardness of the situation. Robert knew too much about my family; I had told him too much, but it was too late.

He was my defender now, my advocate, and his quiet coolness kept my mother's sarcasm at bay. I made animated small talk until he finished his water and stood up to leave.

I can see myself as my mother must have seen us, sitting across from her—an older man, her own age, a handsome, distant, professorial type—and her oldest daughter in short shorts, a tight white knit shirt, long hair down, acting smart and lively and... collegiate. Perhaps for a moment my mother missed the life she might have had, and wondered suddenly whether her daughter, this stranger, was sleeping with this man who was old enough to be her father. The thought would have made her exhausted. *I wash my hands of her, and him,* she might have thought. *She'll survive; she'll be fine.* My mother had worries of her own.

Like a Father

In conversation sometimes, trying to describe Robert, I have said, "He was like a father figure to me then…", as though it will help the listener, as though they would understand something I don't. Robert was old enough to be my father; in fact, he was just a year younger than my father. But I did not want to think of Robert that way, ever.

When I came to college I didn't want to be a daughter to anyone, particularly to my father, who at that time was moving from apartment to apartment and job to job, increasingly unreliable. We couldn't depend on Dad for much, certainly not to tell the truth.

"But Dad," I flippantly confronted him, not long before I went to college, "you *had an affair* with that secretary."

This was in Pueblo, Colorado. I was 15. Dad had come out to the shaded concrete porch where I was lying on a plastic lounger, taking a break from my adolescent efforts to get a suntan. He had been unemployed for a few months by then, "let go" from his latest job as a personnel manager in an office of the Department of Transportation. Mom had left a few days earlier with my brother and sisters, driving to California to stay a while with her mother. The thought of being cooped up in a car with my tedious younger siblings, driving through the southwest in the middle of the summer, was too excruciating.

I stayed behind on the pretense of taking care of our many pets, including an old horse, Chica, that my father had purchased because there was a barn in the backyard. I loved my solitary teenage time—writing poetry, feeding the dog and her puppies, riding and taking care of Chica.

Our road was then at the western edge of town, where the prairie was being excavated for a new subdivision. At night I took late walks and lay down in the middle of the newly paved road, looking up at the stars, enjoying the strange emptiness of the night. I felt excited, full of expectation; I was going to get out of here; my whole life was ahead of me.

The disintegration of our parents' marriage was not perfectly clear to us-their-children, but it seemed my father was primarily to blame, that there had been indiscretions, infidelities. He could not be counted on to hold a job. We knew that just under his joviality was a barely contained anger and, like the animals we were, we sensed he was not dependable.

In the hot shade of the porch, Dad wanted to explain a few things to me about Mom and him. "I did not have an affair," he said to me, his face boiling red, eyes wide and bulging. If he had been a slightly different person he might have slapped me then.

The affair was over, but Dad preferred not to dwell on the truth. He had told himself many stories. My dad then was not someone you could argue with, only someone you could leave behind.

The wave of that bad time crested as I was going off to college. Our house was on the market; my mother had enrolled in nursing school so she could support herself and my sisters. My brother was assigned to live with Dad, and by the time the divorce was final, at the end of the summer I was 17, my father had married his new secretary.

I was eager to be out of the scene of my family's divorce, but I was not really ready to be so independent. I was making-do, and the making-do had a tinge of guilt to it because, even thrust on my own, I knew I had it better than my brother living with my father, or my sisters with Mom, who was panicked, angry, and depressed, spending whole days in her fuzzy yellow bathrobe armed with a Valium prescription. To be on one's own, ready or not, was infinitely better than being with them.

So, Dad dropped me off at Colorado State at the beginning of winter quarter 1975, in the circular driveway in front of the dorm, with my blanket and pillow and typewriter and green canvas Girl Scout duffel bag containing pretty much everything that was mine. I could tell he was uncomfortable and impatient to get back on the road, and I didn't want him checking me into the dorm. I told him to go ahead and go. "Be good now," Dad said, relieved, patting my shoulder before he got back in the car and took off. I saw him again a couple of times when I was in college, again seven years later, and then 20 years passed before we met again. By then I was a grown woman with two children.

What does a daughter need from a father? The father knows his daughter when she is a naked infant and carries that with him; he knows her mess-ups and mishaps, her beautiful growing. He is a sexual being. He made her. As daughters, we want our fathers to be desirable—not to us specifically, but to the world. We want evidence that they are loveable, and that they are lovers. We want them to be both trustworthy and loyal, but also someone to push up against, for in some way that also means that we, too, will be desirable and desired.

I had no role models except what I made up as I went along, trying to find closeness by heading through sex like a dense part of the jungle which, if I was lucky enough, would open out to the place where I'd be loved for my real self. Robert was a place of safety in that jungle. I could try myself out on him, as though he was a father.

And, in whatever way Robert loved me then, during those three years in Fort Collins he did fatherly things for me: he gave me money when I needed it, he helped me move in and out of many apartments, he taught me how to drive his truck and loaned it to me without reservation; he listened to me. Like a father, his love had its judgments—few and far apart, but keenly felt. I was all-revealed to him in the way that a daughter can be all-revealed to her father. Although Robert might disappear for months, he would not retract his love for me, or stop doing things for me because of something I said or did. I knew this.

I could just say he loved me. I loved being loved! I loved myself through his eyes. Doesn't every child need that? (Doesn't every lover want that?) Robert's love was unconditional, not something I had experienced before. I hardly knew what to do with it. I felt I could say or do almost anything I liked and he would be responsive and present.

But did I love him? I thought I did. I accepted our relationship as a kind of mystery that might fall apart if it were analyzed or explained. But perhaps this was obliviousness, not love—the oblivion of a teenager, for that is what I was.

Like a Teacher

If we weren't going to be lovers, then Robert liked the image of himself as a mentor and guide. He was a teacher at heart, pointing me in various directions, feeding me (literally) and keeping me talking, and thinking.

How bold I was in my naivete! The next day after that first dinner and kiss, I slipped drafts of some poems under his office door, which he soon returned to me after class with notes such as: "Save that" or "Is this what you mean?" He had said that he met weekly with a group of friends—a writer, an actress, another philosophy professor. "I told them that perhaps you were the real thing," he said to me, meaning "poet." He thought I was a poet; he wanted that for me and tried to nurture it in me.

Robert bought me two books of poetry that semester—Galway Kinnell's *The Book of Nightmares*, and W.S. Merwin's *The Lice*—which arrived with a letter in my dorm mailbox three weeks after we met:

Saturday, February 14+1, 1975

Gin, here is the poem I mentioned to you a few days ago... It's not your "stuff," certainly not now at any rate, but the style is interesting: He refuses to do the reader's job; each poem demands the reader's participation in determining line breaks, stops, etc. In an engaging way, the reader becomes a partial creator (at least, I think, the invitation is there).

Different readers want their poetry to do different sorts of things. Rightfully, I think. No matter how vast its audience, a poem is always a moving, personal experience. (Not always deeply moving, not always profound—what a bore it would be to lead a profound life—but, still, they always move one). So Merwin's style gets our attention, but more than just a clever experiment, it may also prevent us from remaining too narrow...

Saturday I drove to Boulder to The Brillig Works, a bookstore. A fun place to browse. Or to sit on the floor watching poets, bearded and beardless, budding and broke, copy poems out of books they've been reading. Some Oh's and Ah's, a rhythm to the light in their eyes.

...The Kinnell is wholly deliberate—he gave/took four years to shape it this way—each poem is related to each of the others. A colleague of mine thinks it's necessary to understand them all before we can understand any particular one—he may be right. But it would be a mistake for you to burden yourself with the sort of "stuff" in these poems. Maybe some other time. Nevertheless, note the language. Also there are possibilities for respectable theft. Whatever, just enjoy. Leave Sorrow to Old Men.

The Book of Nightmares, which received rave reviews when it was published in 1971, was indeed too much for me at 17. Ten dark, rich poems about death and fearing death, but also about possibility and new life. And deep solitariness. I could see that in the poems even then, but I didn't understand them; there was a brutality I couldn't take in. So instead I took the gift and, more especially, the attention.

Robert also bought me other new books: Rilke, Annie Dillard, and all of Anne Sexton—hard-bound, because he knew I admired her. No one had given gifts to me so generously before, without expectation. He gave me an image of myself to shape myself against and, flattered and encouraged, I carried and cultivated that identity for a long time. It was something to cling to, and at 17 everything was "potential," both material to write about and a possible someone to be in the world.

Robert's patronage helped me feel more comfortable at the massive state institution. I loved being in college and took a work-study job at the radio station and the newspaper. As soon as I could I found an off-campus apartment and bought a bicycle to get around. After the first boyfriend left me over the summer for his high school girlfriend, I found another boyfriend, older and more mature. I submitted poems to the school magazine and started hanging out with the graduate workshop students. I acted bolder than I was, seeking an identity I could claim.

When I met Robert, he already had an inkling that the university was going to let him go. Enrollment in liberal arts was down. He told me they were laying him off because they wanted someone with a Ph.D. in the position, but really it was because they did not like his proposed doctoral topic on justice. I intuited that his lay-off might be more complicated than that, but we didn't talk about it. I'm sure that his active participation in the Vietnam protests on the conservative campus a few years before didn't help. Once, Robert told me, he had invited the university president to his classroom and let the man "dig himself into a hole" in front of the students over apportioning of the school's budget.

In letters I later found among my own in Robert's apartment were copies of recommendations sent by various colleagues and department heads, both before he came to Colorado State University and as he was being laid off. It was both strange and affirming to read these comments from his past—others had known him!—and I recognized the man they described.

1967 recommendation from W.M., Philosophy Dept, Southern Illinois University
... "Mr. Proctor's problem with us has been his proclivity to procrastination with regard to items leading to the Ph.D. degree. We assume the responsibility for prodding him along on these, however, and believe that he will complete the task in another year or so."

1967 S.M.E., Assoc. Prof. Philosophy, Southern Illinois University
"Mr. Proctor has a good mind. He can argue well. He reads in the field. But he has one great failing. He can never come to any tentative conclusion. He wants to work everything out in detail, have his answer well in hand. Thus, he has a lot of delayed grades...He is not content to hand in a term paper with a conclusion of the moment. He wants it to be a

kind of 'original contribution' to all knowledge. My wife and I have chided him about all this, but to no avail."

1974 A.H.B., Chairman, Philosophy Department Colorado State University

"There is a young man on our staff who did not finish his Ph.D. from Southern Illinois. The administration has constructed an argument from a combination of financial exigency and upgrading faculty which makes his position here untenable. We are leaving no stone unturned in our attempt to find an attractive position he can apply for. He is a very effective teacher and will come with good recommendations."

1979 A.H.B., again

"Although I was not chairman of the Philosophy Department when Mr. Proctor taught here, I got to know him pretty well as a colleague. I was impressed by his obvious success as a classroom teacher, not merely in the sense that the content of his courses was substantial and well prepared, but also in the sense that he was able to create in his students a desire to learn more about philosophy. Students were frequently in his office, not to complain about grades, but to talk more philosophy with him; they came to his house to continue their discussion. I think they saw something rather rare in him, a deep commitment to their education, and they admired him as an example of the best academic traditions… I believe he has the flexibility and a sense of teaching that would make him effective in non-traditional settings with non-traditional students... I believe that there is an untapped reservoir of good students in these non-traditional contexts, I recommend him to you with enthusiasm."

Over the next year of classes, I had two professors who knew Robert. They cluck-clucked at his situation. "Oh," one said, "he's still around?" She did not mean to be harsh, but Robert had a reputation for being a loner—odd, and obstinate in his oddness. His inaction in doing nothing to prevent the university from letting him go, or not completing his doctorate, which was supposedly almost finished, did not make sense to them.

Robert told me that he had $18,000 saved and would be okay for a while. After he was laid off, most days that spring he drove up into the mountains. I don't know what he did; perhaps he hiked, read, sat by the river. He always had a thermos of coffee and a blanket. I went with him a couple of times and we spent the afternoon talking and drinking cheap wine.

For a short time he took a job inventorying books for the campus bookstore. When that ended, he supplemented his savings by making bets at the greyhound track in Denver. At first I didn't believe him when he told me this was how he was spending his evenings, so he took me along one night to the track. He loved the animals, their sleekness and efficiency, and described to me in great detail the qualities of this dog compared to another. It was obvious that he enjoyed it and he was a capable gambler, successful enough to pay the rent for several months.

The university job was the end of Robert's "career." All his jobs since—in a video store, in a video distribution warehouse, in a bookstore—have been loner jobs, paying minimally. He always worked long hours, even when he didn't have to, and he would often complain about how poorly the business was managed, how he had a better system for doing things. Sometimes the employers took his advice; other times they didn't. It was as though each job was all he could do. It was a kind of Artist's Life, without the time or company for creation—without the art.

Although two of my professors advised against it, I left college after my junior year. I was antsy and sick of the routine, full-up of information, and perhaps knew in the back of my head that I could use that last year of school as an incentive later to land somewhere new and finish my degree.

I have no recollection of Robert saying goodbye as I left Fort Collins, although I am sure he did. It probably took a long time, as everything does with him, outside by his truck in front of the broken-down house where I had rented two upstairs rooms. I probably felt impatient, as I often did saying farewell to him. I had my own car, finally; I was ready to move on.

I ended up in Vermont, where I worked two jobs as a secretary and waiting tables in a bar. I hung out with musicians, read my poetry at open-mic evenings. I was aggressively not-a-student. I wrote Robert regularly. Occasionally I called him.

Nov 1977

Robert,

Today after the phone call I gradually got frustrated, then angry, then the whole day was ruined. I should not have called you. #1, you sounded irritated; #2 I did not want to talk poetry. You are becoming the father I love very dearly who, instead of wanting his daughter to be a lawyer, doctor or engineer, wants her to be a poet. Now I'm thinking of it, a hell of a request. And she hits adolescence and rebels. She fears she will lose the approval and contact of her father, at the same time she believes (not "knows") that maybe she has a better idea of what she needs now than he does. She is probably wrong. She will probably discover that when she is 22 or so. Meanwhile, why do daughters always go to fathers and fathers never to daughters?

I can't talk anything but poetry with you, and I want to stay away. Or rather, I don't want pressure. If I have to choose between being a human being who loves and a poet, I'll choose a human being. (Yes, aren't we dramatic.) I feel that school right now would be the worst thing. I have only just entered a different world. (Your response is, "No you haven't. You're delving right back into the same one.") I understand all the whys of it. It would force me to write for more creative writing workshop professors. It would force me to read. I am too young; I am too young; I am too young don't you see I have to step back and look at who I am? Commitment? I don't know if I want to make that commitment. I am just beginning to understand what it's about. You're saying the writing is the only thing I'll ever have a chance at being good at. If I won't wait for myself to catch up with myself, forget it. I will be a <u>housewife.</u>

So there.

For softer talk, I can leave myself open to it. I can at least understand what I am doing when I don't write. Diversions. Who decided I wanted "to write" anyway?

I am past the point at least so that I don't doubt that you love me or that I love you. I feel things. But at this point I am feeling guilty that I will never be what you'd like—and that if I was it'd be too late, etc. I feel like I am supposed to be something for you, to please you, and I am embarrassed that I am not—that I am ridiculous. All my ridiculous pains and lovers and tirades. I am so vulnerable to you I want to hit you.

Ginger

In defiance, still a girl in many ways, I signed my name "Ginger." Robert never called me by that nickname; it was always Virginia.

He wrote back, the only letter from him in the two years that I was in Vermont. It was like his own particular version of Rilke's "Letter to a Young Poet."

February 1978

Virginia,
And the war goes on....
I am glad you don't trust my judgment. Trust your own, believe in your own, rely on your own; it is the only way you can grow. Enough of that too. I don't

much feel like making fatherly, friendly, loverly, uncle-y comments.

Struggles for survival (survival is very chic lately), wars of liberation, revolutions for justice, wars of righteousness all come with the same seal of approval from the same blacksmith's forge. In their name you can justify death, destruction, desolation, alienation, peanut butter, anything at all. There are wars which go on without striving for anything and which no one bothers trying to justify since no one believes in justification any longer. They just, insanely, continue insanely. My war is not like these. It's more like worms and mariposas, only there are no victories.

I've never urged you to become a writer, and certainly not a poet. That is something I thought you wanted. I have urged you to do some things if you want to be a writer, which is quite a different thing... And that is to work at it. It does not matter what you decide to do eventually, but it would make me feel pretty good if you decided and once you decided, you do what is essential for doing it well.

There is something to be learned from the Japanese artist who devotes a life to the very simple tools of a clean piece of paper, a good brush, and good ink. The artist brings imagination, courage, creativity, integrity. If you were religious or spiritually inclined I would tell you to take your life and this medium, your existence, which is only restricted by the limits you place on it, and make it holy.

If you are an artist, make your life free and beautiful.

Someday, perhaps, I'll write you a letter and tell you that I miss you. That sometimes I think of you, intensely, and for long periods (days) not at all.

I wonder what you think of when you look at your favorite picture of yourself. I wonder what you think of yourself—what you think others see and think of you...

Thank you for the letters and phone calls and the things that go with them.

Robert

March 1978

...What do I think of when I look at that picture of myself? I think, yes, that is definitely my mother's big nose. Yes, my dream of long hair is coming true. Yes, this girl is not as hot shit as she used to be but she's okay. I look like a person with life going on inside her. I think that is important, even if I am not that special or incredibly unique, and that is what I think when I see the picture, and why I like it so well.

Am thinking of you, love,

Virginia

Go West, Young Woman
1979

W hen I decided to finish college, and live in a city, I came through Colorado on my way to San Francisco and stayed with Robert for several days. I had told him of my plans, and he gave me $300 and the name of a former student, friend, and fellow war protestor who lived in Berkeley. I was very grateful for them both; Robert's friend became a place to stay for a couple of weeks, and the money was the deposit on a studio apartment in the Civic Center area of San Francisco.

I have called those first days in San Francisco my "Mary-Tyler-Moore days," recalling the opening image at the beginning of the 1970s television show, where Mary has moved to Minneapolis and, in a moment of excitement and exuberance at all the possibilities of her life, surrounded by the bustle of the big city, she tosses her beret high into the air. That was how it felt to be in San Francisco then. My college Spanish had gotten me a break in the rent on my apartment in the Civic Center, and each day I took the streetcar downtown in the morning fog to this temp job or that.

The city in 1979 seemed safe and accessible for a young woman, teeming with interesting people. I got up each morning feeling eager to belong. One afternoon during the first month there I had the radio on to a live report on the aftermath of the trial of Dan White, who had been arrested and then acquitted for murdering city council member Harvey Milk and Mayor George Moscone. I turned the radio off, but the sound continued—the protests were happening just a block outside my apartment. Living among so many people it was easier to believe that plot existed, and I was part of it.

That spring I experienced my first earthquake, too, just a small one—a deep shaking as though a truck had crashed into the building. Neighbors opened their windows to the back alleyway to see if the street had cracked, and there was an odd moment of camaraderie as we waved at each other before going back to our separate worlds.

In the evenings I took a class at San Francisco State University, a seminar on T.S. Eliot, where I met John. Oh, I was bored with Eliot, having spent probably too much time reading his poetry at college in Colorado. I was late enrolling; I signed up because it was one of only a few classes still open. John took it because he was beginning to read poetry and short stories and had fallen in love with *Four Quartets*. He had had a number of majors, including music and history, and most recently English. He asked me out a few times before I finally accepted, after the last class of the semester. I hesitated, thinking he might be gay. (For those first few months in the city every man seemed gay to me; I was awed and amazed by the pierced, flamboyant, leather chaps-wearing men in the Market Street Safeway.)

John was urban—I see him in his crisp, white shirt tucked into slacks, bare feet in clogs, a trimmed beard and his vivid, beautiful blue eyes. He had a kind of relaxed animation, an independent liveliness, his coolness blended just-so. He worked part-time and went to school part-time, not in a hurry to do or be anything. If the possibility to take a trip came up, he would empty his savings account and travel. He loved San Francisco and knew where to go. I think of the simple, black-banded watch on his left wrist; his wide, competent hands. This was a man who might love me, but not overwhelm me with that love.

John has said that when he thinks of me then he sees a slender woman in jeans with unfashionable seams in them, flannel button-down shirts, desert boots, and long, red, wild hair. My cheap jeans and unfeminine shirts projected a certain deliberate, intelligent nonchalance. Besides my hair, he was attracted to my straightforward remarks, my apparent self-sufficiency, my intensity. I was not cool; I was not urban; I seemed to be who I was, and he liked that.

We began spending every weekend together. Weeknights, too, sometimes.

Like a Friend

Robert and I talked on the phone many times after I first arrived in San Francisco. I knew he would love this city, now my turf, and I cajoled him to come for a visit. In my plans, I would be the one showing *him* around. We would go to the usual amazing sites—Golden Gate Park, Ocean Beach, the Cliff House, Muir Woods—and then eat *huevos rancheros* at the joint on 14th Street. He accepted my invitation and drove the thousand miles from Colorado, arriving in the yellow truck with a Nevada suntan and patched jeans. He stayed with me in my studio apartment for two weeks, sleeping on the floor, taking long walks all over the city while I went to my receptionist job downtown.

I was anxious for John and Robert to meet and had spoken extensively about each of them to the other. Who knows what I said? "There's this weird man in my life. He's older. He used to be a teacher of mine in college. No, we never slept together." About John: "He's really great. He's just starting to write short stories. We met in my T.S. Eliot class."

One Saturday afternoon during Robert's visit, I made a plan to bring them together. We met at Finnegan's Wake on 24th Street. John was sitting at the dark bar, a Guinness in hand, one eye on the TV, half on and half off the bar stool in his tall, lanky way, a wired, attractive casualness in all his movements. What if John was suspicious of Robert, or Robert put on his cold self, as he had done when he met my mother? I introduced them; it was an instant simpatico. I could see that they might even be friends without me—a relief—and they were. From that first meeting, John was never jealous of my friendship with Robert. Perhaps in those early days the complications of the relationship made me seem more interesting. Then, as Robert engaged him over time, honing in on John's interests in that way he had, getting him to talk about writing and travelling and music, the two became friends and went out together on their own. Always, even in his intensity, Robert was "other" enough to not seem threatening to John.

At Finnegan's Wake, we moved from the bar to a table, and had dinner.

There was such easiness and awkwardness in that visit from Robert. Something in our relationship had shifted, no longer mentor-student. I had grown up. When he would sometimes look at me in that certain intense way, I was uncomfortable and acted casual to keep his tenderness from swallowing me.

He was more willing than before to talk, to be openly confused about his life, and in those two weeks of his visit we conjured up the possibility that perhaps he might move to San Francisco. There was nothing holding him in Colorado, no good job or friends or obligations, and after a few months and several more phone calls he decided he would come. It was time for something new, he said. I remember feeling positive; perhaps proximity would ease the awkwardness. I longed for him to be my friend in a new way. Before coming, he wrote me an ebullient letter:

> *September 1979*
>
> *Virginia,*
> *It's difficult writing. I'm not accustomed to letting go in the way you are. And it's complicated by the way I feel about you; it's as though each word, each sentence is just too damned important...*
> *The long & wide of it is that you are too close just now. It is not at all like thinking about you; more like carrying your eyes next to mine when I look at anything. And I go around with your voice swimming in the hollow of my ear, your hair stitching the back of my neck.*
> *All this to say that I had a fantastic two weeks, to say I miss you, to say you are noticeably absent. Ah, I'm lucky we're just the best of friends.*
> *You now have incontrovertible proof that insanity is not inherited. That would give genetics too much credit. It takes a lot of hard work to get to where I am.*

...My plans are quite indefinite as to how soon I will get a job or what sort of job I will get. I think I will take quite a long while for myself before I go back to work. I want to reassess some things: mostly I want to study a while and get back to writing and reading. And I have some ideas for going back to school, partly to <u>retrain</u> for some things I'm getting excited about wanting to try—I'll tell you about this later...

For what it's worth, you've made me feel hopeful and alive for a change...We will have some talk, you and I, about our current apathy, and we'll have you writing and reading again, shortly. We will get each other going again. Mope if you like, you only have a few more weeks to do so.

How dare you put me in the "precarious friends" category. There are ties just as strong as umbilical cords; they are not precarious friends.

Where was I? Oh yes! I have a great love for you, which makes me happy enough to offer to buy dinner at Pings. But only if you continue to eat like a bird.

Much love to you

Robert

Though I loved his letter, where he was revealed without interruption from me, it made me nervous. He sounded extremely happy, more exuberant than I had ever heard before, and a couple of weeks later he arrived in San Francisco again, his truck packed with all those familiar boxes of books. He slept on the couch in the flat my sister Carolyn and I had rented together on Fairmount Street when she had moved to the city.

That November, Carolyn and I hosted Thanksgiving at the flat and my mother, brother, and other sister all came up from

Southern California where they were now living. It was the first time we had been together in a long time. John took artsy black-and-white photos of each of us on the couch. Robert was in charge of the broccoli, his favorite vegetable, and we teased him about his careful preparation. He had purchased far too much, and he carefully washed and dried each stalk before mincing it. By now, he was a figure in my family's lives, too, and this was the first of many crazy Thanksgivings together as each of my siblings and my mother moved to the Bay Area.

As the days went by, it was close quarters in the flat; Robert's presence was heavy, and in the nine weeks he stayed with us it was hard to tell whether he was really looking for a job or a place to live. Eventually, he found an apartment close by, on Valley Street, behind a real estate office—a great deal for its low rent and location. The dark brown walls of the apartment absorbed the little light there was. We offered to help paint the place? It never happened. His boxes stacked up against the wall, as before; a kitchen table with a couple of chairs; and his mattress on the floor, tightly made as usual.

Robert found a job as a clerk in a video warehouse. He was settled, and I was relieved. In the city there were hundreds of places to meet for our long dinners. Maybe that was the best way for us to be friends.

Women

Robert was married, twice. The first was Jane, in Chicago, in 1961. They were in their mid-20s. Did they meet in school? What did she look like? She was studying opera, and he was in graduate school. Her family didn't like him much, he said. Neither of them cared about marriage, but her family did, so they had a traditional church wedding.

"We just handed it all over to them."

They had great sex. "Sometimes we just screwed, right on the stairs." It sounded strange to hear him say this.

They both loved music and attended a lot of concerts. Together, they listened to recordings, analyzing voices. He helped Jane with her singing, advising her where to push it, when to back off. I once asked him whether she liked this advice. Robert said he thought so. But I wondered if maybe she didn't like it—maybe it became a one-way relationship—all the work on and about her.

Then he had an opportunity for the teaching job at Colorado State and he took it while Jane stayed behind. She was becoming a good singer and she, too, had opportunities, but they were in Chicago. She came out to visit a few times and they took long drives and hikes, but her heart wasn't in it. After a year of being apart, without notice, she mailed him divorce papers. When the surprise waned, Robert completed them and sent them back.

"I didn't contest it. We didn't even really talk about it. There wasn't anything for me there, or anything for her here... It just seemed impossible. But I should have fought for our relationship. I should have done something," he told me later.

Sometime during his decade at Colorado State he met Sherri, a veterinary student, and they moved in together. He married her, he said, because her daughter needed medical insurance, which they could get through his employment at the university. When a friend of Robert's moved in with them, Sherri fell in love with him. They kept the rented house, and Robert moved out.

Many years later, in the city, he heard that Sherri had committed suicide.

There were possibly other women in those years.

For six weeks Robert and a friend of mine were lovers. Kristine had come out to San Francisco for a week to visit me in the city. We had been in a class together, and she had known Robert from the college, where she was a secretary. During her visit she and Robert spent time together taking walks, having coffee, and doing city-things while I was at work. The three of us had dinner at my place the night before she was leaving. My apartment was small and cozy, with two doorless rooms and a kitchenette. I had to get up early and eventually I set up my futon in the bedroom. Whispering, Kristine asked me if I minded if Robert stayed over.

I did mind, but I said I didn't.

I heard them laugh quietly and whisper in the other room, then the squeak of the couch, the sounds of kissing. My hearing became acute. I turned over loudly, a reminder that I was just in the other room. Just go to his place, I was thinking, but ever-so-polite, I did not get up and say so. I felt strangely excluded, but left out more like a child than a lover. Fully awake, I listened to the muffled cries, the sound of more kisses and sighs—private sighs.

Within a month, Robert made the trip in his truck to get Kristine and her belongings, and she moved in with him.

So, briefly, we were two couples—John and I, Robert and Kristine. We went out often, for drinks and dinner, movies, to museums. In spite of the awkward night during her visit, I was eager to see Robert in a different way. Kristine wanted an intimate relationship badly and she must have been very optimistic. In the dark apartment, she tried to make a home with him; she cleaned the place, unpacked his books. She shopped, made meals. We even went over there once for dinner, the only time I ever ate a sit-down dinner in a place where he lived. It was hard to tell whether Robert was happy; he seemed to do what he was asked to do. But that was his way.

Then one afternoon Kristine came over to say she didn't think it was working out. Robert was always giving to her; he didn't know how to receive. "He's always asking what do I want—he doesn't have a clue what he wants." Another thing, she said, he was so slow—it was driving her crazy, the time it took to get dressed, to get the truck warmed up, to eat… "Sometimes I'll wake up and he's sitting in the chair by the bed just watching me, just looking at me. It weirds me out." We both saw the impossibility of what she had tried.

In his careful way, Robert again packed the truck; they hugged goodbye, and this time I drove Kristine back to

Colorado, towing her car behind. She had been gone less than two months. After that my friendship with her drifted.

He soon met another young woman at his work, Diane. Her name began coming up regularly in our conversations. Robert had long dinners with her, as he had with me, and he told me that Diane wanted to meet me. It felt like a challenge. I was curious, and joined the two of them at the diner on 24th Street. They had arrived before I did. Had they come together? I sat in the booth next to Robert. Diane was slender, with dark curly hair. Sitting across from her, I could feel why Robert was attracted to her. I could not help the comparisons. Diane was smart and sensual alongside my bright-eyed, confessional self. There was a directness in the way she flirted with both Robert and me. Jealousy and relief were completely mixed in my response to her. Eventually I left them to continue their leisurely conversation without me.

Later I asked Robert whether they were sleeping together, and he said no. Diane had a boyfriend, but their relationship was troubled; Robert was a concerned, protective confidant for her—his most comfortable role with women.

A few months later at one of our breakfasts together, Robert told me that he had been in love with Diane, and feeling that way had at least made him realize how "foolish" he'd been for so long, what he might have had if he had given himself the chance. There might have been a woman for him. The statement startled me; it was the first time I had heard Robert say something so clearly, without regret. I didn't try and tell him, Oh, it might still work out with someone, because for many people there was a good chance it would never work out with anyone. What did you do after you realized that?

Years later he told me, "There was a time when Diane wanted a relationship with me. We were spending more and more time with each other. I think we would have been good together. She wanted to have a child, and she invited me. But I said no. It was too late. I didn't want to get into that business again."

My Tendency is to Run
1981

R obert and I barely spoke of the two months with my friend Kristine, as though it didn't happen. But the relationship was a rift between us. All his inadequacies and his refusal or inability to deal with them had risen to the surface. For his part, since Kristine was my friend, perhaps he felt set up. I was angry; he was angry. On a phone call, he was sharp in his criticism of a story I had sent to him to read, and I hung up on him. Over two months where we did not see each other, we wrote letters. I received half of the 10 or so letters I have ever received from him in that short, broken stretch of time. In his sprawling script, he talked to me on yellow-lined legal paper more clearly, more straightforwardly, than he ever had. I have held onto his letters like some kind of map, something to ground the two of us, rare physical evidence of his side of our friendship.

5/5

Dear Virginia,
I was wrong the other day, and never should have said anything in anger...
Your letter arrived this afternoon. I read it, then went for a run, and read it again while having dinner.

By now, the juices are working on it, breaking it down into cellular size bites so that I can digest it. I think it one of the best letters you've ever written. But, aside from that, I agree with the sense of it, the tone and spirit of it, the truth of it. I sent a letter to Kristine this week; not a good letter, written, I would now guess, with a little anger, and I'd like to repeat some of it. It won't be exact, but it'll do.

Emotionally, psychologically, spiritually— whatever—I'm more than a little messed up. The facts that contribute to this are simple enough; I'm broke, I need a job, I've made another failed "relationship." But that is only the fun part. The not so fun part has been the weeks of criticism, by others and by myself. The short of it is that whatever little ego I may have had left has not merely been deflated but flattened. It's just no fun at all knowing that your friends know you are full of guilt and have little self-worth, that, in fact, I'm boring and terribly uncomfortable to be with; so much so, they'd rather avoid me. And I'm humiliated.

So I've had enough "the trouble with you, Robert" for a while. In fact, I'm going on a long diet...

My tendency is to run. But I won't. (Though, I can <u>see</u> myself running across the flat plain of a prairie or a desert, heading east into the low hills just at dawn, the sun dead red on the rise.) I won't run, but a vacation is in order. So I think it might help (or be necessary, even), if we didn't pressure each other for a while, anyway; and that means not seeing each other...

In the meantime, I've started a running, reconditioning program... So if I complete the 12 weeks

*I'll be back in fairly good running condition. I might
even lose some of my pot belly. All of this involves
relearning... Perhaps there'll be emotional relearning.*

*What I liked about your letter was its care, every-
thing mattered. You are developing a wonderful
gentleness in your aged condition.... I expect more
from you than you think you are capable of, so I'm not
fair at all sometimes.*

I love you both.

Robert

A month later he pulled a muscle and had to stop his
running regime. He ran out of money; I sent him a check.

6/26

Dear R—

...I drive by your place occasionally, but I only get
angry. This is not to say I don't love you, ever, but
that I don't know if your staying away is going to
help the anger. (Whose? yours or mine?) May only
aggravate it. I get tired of your romance. And there
may be nothing to do about that but go on.

Oh, etc.

V

6/27

Virginia,

*Why are you angry? It might help for you to say it
outright. I'm angry about me, not with the world or
with anyone else. But that's not why I stay away, at
most it is just another small weight added to an
already unbalanced personality... Why is a normally*

intelligent, physically healthy person always doing foolish, even stupid things? Why do I manage to destroy anything of value I've ever known?...And I feel terrible thinking that you think less of me.

Is that tactless? Is it too much pressure?...

Sometimes I think that what I need is for you to be me for a few days and me you. I would talk and you would listen and be able to tell me what the hell is going on. You would be astonished by my dreams.

I'm thinking about John as a reason not to write and while it is so, it is not so simple...

Thank you for writing. I often wonder what you had dreamt or thought during a day. Recently I dreamed an accident in which no one was hurt. That gave me a chance to ask, "How are you?" "The weight fell on me," you said. And I wondered how you were for several days. What weight? Me, I suppose.

R

7/1

R,

   I'm angry because you are angry with yourself and refuse to <u>give</u> any part of that anger to the world and people around you. Thus, you nurse it. Thus, you're delicate. And everyone has to treat you so damn delicately... Your romance, I guess, is your "inability."

   ...If you would let people care about you <u>in the way that they can.</u> So often it seems like it's just not enough. That your gaps WILL NEVER BE FILLED and therefore nothing makes any difference. "Friends" feel guilty somehow, having failed to fill gaps. So of course you're "friendless"...

V

6/28, 7/5

Virginia,

...I want so much to be honest with you, to be honest with myself; it's the same thing really. But old habits are hard to throw off, and the disguises (so clever, at times), because of all the fears, are even more difficult to get through. My language is a terrible one. It's so damned hard to say anything simply, straightforwardly without the overbearing weight of "learned" correctness. Everything I say is pretentious, grandiloquent and abstract, deliberately mystifying in order to be impressive. So my thinking fails me when I need it most, because my language fails. That's how deep the lie goes; how ingrained, how awful it is. These very lines are part of it.

So it isn't that I don't want to respond to your openness or to the love you offer or to the opportunities and urging you give, but it's frightening and complicated and a lot more. But enough of this...

You are right about a lot of things, as usual...that I need help and that it shouldn't be you. It bothers me a lot that I don't know how to love people and don't know how to allow them to love back. And, of course, I do not allow, as you say, people to care for me in the way that they can. I feel terrible about things like this because I think they are the sort of things I should know about in some positive way, that I should be able to help someone not the other way around...

I have been thinking a very long time about your writing... Delacroix said "To be a poet at 20 is to be 20, to be a poet at 40 is to be a poet." Consider that you've passed 20, that you do the only things anyone can do; you live and think about that, you read and think about that, you write and think about that; that you have already learned that what you need is direction, not movement; that you already know there are a good many sheerly technical problems that have to be learned so that you can handle them; that though you write for your own pleasure (as well as others) and think it adds to your significance as a person, you write mostly to fulfill a need to write; that you already know that there is no achievement only achieving and that it will take a long, long, long time; that you have talent you are responsible for—feed it with life and thought and writing and reading like everyone else before you has done (as you well know) and it will grow; that there is and can be no time limit—you may put it aside because it is not your time, you may put it aside for years, but you cannot put it away. Consider this for a while, go on reading, go on writing, whatever you can when you can, go on thinking, go on bitching about it, but go on.

I have been thinking for over a year now that it might be a very good idea for me to read over what you have done, to see what themes and concerns and ideas keep coming out, and in this way perhaps find some direction in what you have done, not ought to do. But it would take a while and a lot of careful effort...

To be a creator is virtually a demand to be recognized as one. You can justifiably be proud of what you have created...

I'm not always so delicate, more hard-headed and stupid than anything else. I do not know how to stop being this way, and certainly I do not even know how to begin in any positive way to being the sort of person

who is giving in the way you are. That is a reason for
getting some help, because I really don't understand
very much, and, in my case, I seem unable to change
without some sort of understanding.

I know this is late, but send me the poems anyway,
and thanks,

R

Now, I am older than he was when he wrote the letters, and they have become precious to me. Here was the friendship— on the edge of self-pity, of romantic longing, still nuanced with fatherly, teacherly advice, but shifted, opened-up in a way that had rarely happened since. He revealed himself and re-revealed himself. He was running, but didn't run away. So many years later, I wanted to read each of them to him and say, *See! you know yourself! how clearly you see yourself, how honest and straightforwardly you speak!* I'd say, *Why can't you talk like this now?* Always wanting something more from him.

"It bothers me a lot that I don't know how to love people and don't know how to allow them to love back. And, of course, I do not allow, as you say, people to care for me in the way that they can."

But this was it—this was the talk through which he could allow someone to love him. They would love, as I do, the plainness in it, the reality, the striving. The sadness, even. Wouldn't they say, "Who is this man who knows himself so well, who seems so kind, so real, so loving? I want to know him."

In his letters he described an obvious clinical depression; he even recognized the need for help that could not be me. So why didn't he ever get help? Why didn't he?

Even then I sometimes thought with a piercing dismay that all these go-rounds, these depressive cycles, my anger, his disappearing, all these wasted months and years in our friendship might have been alleviated, or significantly different, with the help of a prescription and a regular appointment with a good therapist—something...simple! Robert would step in front of a bus for me, but he wouldn't seek treatment for depression. He would not let himself be helped. That was, to me, the Biggest Sin; that was the stone wall, the great pit.

If I were him for a few days, and he were me, as he suggested, what world would I have seen from his dark rooms behind the real estate agent's office? Would he, seeing me/himself there, have been able to help me/himself? What would he have done? Where I was full of *shoulds*, his love for me was unconditional. Would he have showered that unconditional love on me and saved me? Or would he, like me, suggest therapy and medication? It is very romantic to go down and be saved for a while and then go down again. But this was tiresome, this was serious; this was even dangerous.

Hello! I say to myself now. *This is mental illness!* I did not understand the cycles of hope and plans, despair, and disappearance. The tedious repetitions. How did we not know it? The fact was, we knew a lot of people who were diagnosable in those days. I was working in the office of a mental health clinic at that time, entering intakes and diagnoses into a database every day, interacting with counselors and their clients. But in his depression or his delusions, Robert never went over any edges, never acted out (at least in front of us or others), and kept the jobs he had (indeed, over-functioned at them) for a long time. More to the point, he never noted or acknowledged things were not right with him. These letters were the first time.

Then, through a friend of mine, he got another job as a clerk in a video store and the stress (and the revelation) receded.

De Haro Street

Later the next summer, John and I found a place to rent together, a house that could rightfully be called "charming," nestled on a 25-by-100 foot hillside lot along a straggly one-way section of De Haro Street. Occasionally we saw the house in the background on reruns of the TV show "The Streets of San Francisco"—a pitched-roof, white clapboard, child's-drawing-of-a-house all alone on a hill behind the cop cars bouncing over unpaved roads in the sunny outskirts neighborhood that was Potrero Hill then, before houses and condominiums filled the block. It was built in the 1930s, a simple out-of-the-way cottage which later became a hippie house. Several times we came home to find some stranger standing outside on the sidewalk, gazing at the building: "I crashed here once for a few months..." "I remember some really great parties here..." It was a funky, intimate house, with lots of leaks and creaks, and no insulation. A wall of reclaimed post office boxes separated the bathroom and sunroom, which had been converted from a porch on the back of the house.

Oh, the view from that sunroom! We had our café table there and watched the sun going down behind Sutro Tower, the billowing fog getting tangled on Twin Peaks, two tips of the Golden Gate Bridge visible toward the north. The back door from the porch led down two flights on a rickety spiral staircase to a tiered backyard with a big willow tree on a postage-stamp of grass and a small old brick patio, then further down concrete-fashioned steps with small shrubs, jade trees, and other succulents, to another small patch of dirt at the bottom by the fence. It looked inviting but was usually too cool and shadowy in the mornings and too windy in the afternoons to sit out there.

When John and I first rented De Haro, astonished at our good luck and the cheap rent, the owner's brother-in-law lived in the unit beneath us, and we soon discovered that patience was part of our discounted rent. "Red," a big man with long sideburns, aviator glasses and red hair, was a gardener for the city, and brought home plants and maintained the terraced backyard. He drove a huge red El Dorado for which he claimed a parking space directly in front of the house. The only light for the in-law unit was through the big west windows in the small kitchen, but Red made his rent-free apartment cozy. He bought a piano and we lived through two years of his tinkling George Winston-like improvisations, along with occasional rages about the shared heat being turned up too high or our feet clomping too heavily across his ceiling.

The long living room was carpeted, but the other rooms had wide-plank floors. There was a minimal kitchen with open shelves for dishes. John refinished an old oar as a handrail for the narrow stairway leading to two angled-roof bedrooms upstairs. It was cold in the winter, and sometimes in the summer, when the wind and fog finally blew across the city from Twin Peaks. John constructed big storm windows out of plexiglass, which we affixed to the leaky windows with industrial velcro. On the street side, he built an office for us with two desks adjacent the windows and added a door to close off the room. I was completing my bachelor's degree, one credit at a time. John was finishing his master's degree and teaching at a private alternative high school in the East Bay.

We were immersed in our "post-hippie, pre-yuppie" life, as my sister called it. We decided to have a baby. I got pregnant. We got married at City Hall. Robert bought two cases of wine for the party, to which he did not come.

There are stretches of our lives that are physically branded into us, for whatever reason, and those first years at De Haro were a time like that for me, the house like a character in our plot. I don't think of that time without wandering through the rooms of that house, feeling its drafts, smelling garlic and coffee; hiking up the steep cobblestones of 24th Street, the sound of Highway 101 like a river down the hill; watching the fog swell toward us in slow motion; the spikey pink blossoms of the bottle-brush trees in front of the house, smelling the fennel across the road when I opened the front door, feeling the weight of the baby inside me. The house was in my body like the pregnancy, and just as I still occasionally dream that I am pregnant, I also dream of De Haro, usually discovering rooms that I didn't know existed.

John built a changing table, which I painted a couple of days before our son Kevin was born, in September 1983, at San Francisco General. We could see the hospital from the sun porch window.

A Fine Day
1983

What was a fine day with Robert? Certainly there have been many fine days with him, mornings until late at night. Days without hurry or agenda. When I was in college in Fort Collins, we would drive up the Poudre River and park somewhere. He'd warm up the yellow Ford, taking his time, making sure I had a sweatshirt or sweater (just in case), put a couple of apples and peanut butter sandwiches into a bag, Coke for me, coffee into a thermos for him, and off we'd go. One time, sitting languidly on a boulder by the river, we saw a goshawk. Another time, some deer. We didn't listen to music; it was noisy in the big truck, and not easy to drive. I can see the heel of Robert's hand as he gently guided the giant knob of the stick shift into gear.

A few years later when he moved to San Francisco I did most of the driving in my VW. Several times we took the Muni bus and then the ferry to Angel Island and spent the day. We would find ourselves a picnic spot and then go roaming together or separately on the roads and paths around the island, always with the Bay in view. There was one magnificent day there with John and Kristine. Robert and I went on a walk, lost track of the time, and had to race to make the last ferry, laughing and out of breath. I saw John from the ferry deck, waving. Robert-the-runner jogged ahead down the hill toward the dock, arms raised as in a victory lap, laughing. Had I ever seen him laugh like that? The boat blasted its horn at us; the passengers clapped as we boarded. And the evening was still ahead; we would have a cheap dinner somewhere, and drink, and laugh some more. Part of the fineness of the day was feeling this time stretching out in front of us.

When it was just the two of us, the day would be filled with talk punctuated with silence and sometime brief naps (by me). I needed the nap because I did most of the talking. Robert would ask questions, check in with me like a parent, and encourage me to analyze and ramble through my relationships, my writing struggles, my plans. We both enjoyed the drive, the walk, the view, the pleasure of being out somewhere different. We noticed the same things and could tell that we were noticing with just a glance at each other, or a word or two.

Even in 40 years, there have really been only about 20 of these long days together, the content of which I have forgotten, remembering just the feeling of affection and open-ended time.

We spent one fine day together in early September of 1983, just before Kevin was born, leaving late in the morning to go to St. Mary's College in the East Bay. I wanted to put up flyers advertising my word processing business, which I was starting in anticipation of being home with the baby. Robert had loaned me a chunk of money; I registered myself as a business and bought one of the new IBM personal computers and software. Under the blue cotton maternity dress my big pregnant belly twisted and squirmed as we walked the peaceful campus. We talked about the baby, what having a child would be like, and my new business. Over a late lunch, we talked about my mother, who had recently moved up from Southern California to be nearer to me and my sisters and was living in a mobile home in Santa Rosa. She was going to help me out for a couple of weeks after the baby was born. After lunch, Robert didn't feel well. We were unaccustomed to the summer heat of the East Bay.

Two weeks later, I gave birth to a baby boy. Robert arrived at the hospital hours after he was born, holding him outstretched, examining the strange vessel of life that a newborn is, and baby Kevin sneezed ferociously several times.

"You should have someone look into that," I remember Robert saying, his carefulness revealed in a new arena.

False Spring
1984

A few months after Kevin was born, Robert checked into the hospital for the second time to investigate a chest pain he had been having on and off for a month. The cardiogram was abnormal. It could be as simple as a valve infection, the doctors said, or as complex as a blocked artery, which would require surgery. Robert prepared for the worst.

Before he went into the hospital I invited some people for a surprise breakfast celebration of his 51st birthday, including Diane and some of his co-workers from the video warehouse where he was working. The breakfast at the diner on 24th Street was a little awkward—to be expected with such different people and Robert being who he was—but he seemed happy to be celebrated. Afterward, he spent the afternoon with me before John was going to drive him to the hospital. We took a long walk over Potrero Hill to the industrial area down by what was then Todd Shipyards, strangely quiet and empty on Sunday, no ships in dry dock. At the Mission Rock Resort, I had a hamburger and a beer and Robert sipped coffee.

It was February, false spring in the Bay Area. Finches did their singing dance on the telephone wires by the playground. On the wooden stairs coming back up the hill, a plum tree, deceived, had blossomed. Crossing the bridge over I-280, I thought how I had a son at home, and for the first time since he was born I had gone a whole hour without thinking of him. The clouds hung low and inlandish, getting cooler as the ones coming over Twin Peaks turned to fog. We walked slowly, painstakingly careful because of his heart. I felt edgy. Our conversation went in familiar stops and starts. I was 26; I had known Robert a third of my life; I couldn't imagine losing him, or him not being in the back of my mind. He had been back there so long that I hardly noticed him anymore.

Perhaps because he was going into the hospital, he wanted to talk, to tell me "everything," if that were possible, or even necessary. Here's my guess of what he wanted to say: he wanted to tell me how much he loved me—and Diane, too. Perhaps he wanted to apologize for having been absent from us and himself for a long time. But if that was what he wanted to say, it was not what he said. Instead, he recounted a conversation with someone at work, spoke professorially of how the demographics of the city would dramatically change in the next few years....

John took him to the hospital. After an overnight stay, the tests concluded that the indigestion Robert had felt on the day we went to the East Bay had been a mild heart attack. He was okay; there was nothing to be done, but he would have to be careful for a while.

Underneath Us
1985

T he Potrero Hill neighborhood where we were living was up-and-coming. When we had first moved into De Haro, construction was being completed on a set of expensive three-story condominiums flush against our house on one side. Knowing he could cash in, the owner decided to sell our house and gave us the first option to buy, offering to personally finance us at the market interest rate. He knew we were reliable rent-payers who would probably translate into reliable mortgage-payers. John and I had no credit; we had not thought of our future beyond having the baby and John getting his teaching job, so this was an exciting option. But we needed a down payment and someone to rent the downstairs apartment. Robert came to mind. If we split the mortgage and utilities three ways, it would be only slightly more than we had paid for rent. We borrowed money from John's brother and my mother, and Robert, amazingly, came up with the balance. A creative exchange was made; Red moved into Robert's apartment on Valley Street, and Robert moved into the downstairs apartment.

Suddenly, we-three were homeowners.

For his share of the money, Robert had contacted his brother, with whom he owned a piece of property that they sold. A brother? We had never heard of one. Richard was maybe eight years older than Robert. Catholic. Married with nine children.

I suppose we had always speculated that Robert had a "secret" life, but this was the first physical evidence of it. All these years we hadn't asked; he didn't tell—an omission on his part, or a failure of interest on ours? I felt odd about this new information, in the same way I did when Robert told me that sometimes he would stroll the galleries in the chic section of the city, in his worst running clothes. Gallery owners thought he was a wealthy eccentric. By inquiring in a certain tone, he said, he would get himself shown to the "back room" where the more interesting pieces were. It sounded like Robert enjoyed the joke he was playing on them at least as much as seeing the exclusive paintings.

We were excited about buying the house together, amazed at our own good fortunes. Like all Robert's past dwellings, the in-law apartment that had been Red's had a lower level entrance off the street, but it opened in the back to a deck and the eclectic backyard and the western sun. We talked about how he could change this or that; he could paint the bathroom or replace the stove. He would be close by. What a wonderful thing for friends to live together! As John helped Robert move his boxes from the truck into the downstairs apartment, Kevin, now almost 2, called out to him in excitement, "Bob-o! Bob-o!", his special name for Robert, who always laughed when he heard Kevin's chortle.

After he moved in, we did not go into his apartment again for the next two and a half years that we lived there. He stopped knocking on our door after about a month. Then there were several months of silence, or a brief hello if we ran into each other on the back staircase, coming up from the laundry room, or going down. We heard nothing from downstairs except the door opening and closing, sometimes water running in his kitchen. It was the same life he had lived in every other place, except now we were living on top of him. John and I were in our new-parent world, our concerns wrapped tightly around employment, daycare, each other. We remembered Robert, we forgot him. We tried to get Kevin to run softer up and down the hallway.

His presence was an absence; his absence was a presence. What was the point of living with him, near him, if we didn't connect? It would have been better if he were a stranger renting from us.

Once during that time our paths crossed as Robert was getting in his truck to go to work. Did I go up to him, or did he call out to me? Did he have some practical matter to relate? He rolled down the window. I remember trying to peel away that sheet of bad silence between us, as I usually did.

"So, Robert, what's going on? You've disappeared."

He shrugged. "I'm thinking it might be best if I left here for a while."

I didn't know what to say. He was getting ready to drive off somewhere and it had been too long since we last talked. I stood awkwardly by the truck. "We'll find you," I said.

And he said, almost proudly, "No. You won't."

His Story

Robert was born in Illinois on February 7, 1933. For years I thought his middle name was John, but it is James. I also thought he was born a year later, in 1934. He never corrected me. I'd been on my own with his story.

A few years ago I told him I was writing about us. "I'm writing about you and me, and our friendship," I said. He was quiet for a moment or two, and if he was surprised or perturbed there was no indication of it. Then he asked, "Do you need anything from me?"

It took a moment for me to realize by "anything" he meant letters or poems I had sent him. "Not now," I said. I took the query to be his approval of the project.

What he could have said, but didn't, was, "What will you say about us? You don't even know me." So I told him I needed to meet with him, to have one or more of our long dinners, and hear about his childhood. He treated our dinner dates as a serious endeavor, and I think he was secretly pleased to have this attention officially directed his way. They were not easy evenings. The first night I tried to just listen and take occasional notes. At the second meeting, I was my friendly, least-favorite, administrative self, redirecting him over and again to the question I had asked in order to get an answer. He drifted and wavered. This is not a transcript, but close to what he told me:

My mother was Mary Deering. My father was Arthur Proctor. He was a fireman, and he left the family when I was two. I have no idea why. It was never discussed.

I had a sister, Mary Ann, who was six years older than me, and a brother, Richard, who was four-and-a-half years older. There was another child, Daniel, born before me, who died. I pray for him now.

After my father left, I lived for two years with my aunt. My brother and sister were sent to St. Mary's Training School in Des Plaines.

When I was 5, I remember walking up a hill with Mother and watching a train coming across some tracks. Past that there was the library, and a cab company, and we took a cab to a home where there were other small children. I remember simply going somewhere, and I counted the traffic lights and told myself I would remember the number so I could get back home. It wasn't far, not more than two or three miles from where my mother lived, but I don't remember her visiting. It was actually a small farm. I remember liking living there. I could walk around. There were gardens, fruit trees—apples, maybe—barns. There were chickens. I remember a chicken being killed and boiling it in water to get the feathers off.

I remember hearing Roosevelt announce World War II on the radio. We made a lot of balsa wood airplanes and set them on fire and dropped them off the barn roof.

When I was 7, I was also sent to St. Mary's where my brother still lived and went to school. My sister was older and was with my mother again then. St. Mary's was 10 or so miles away. There were 30 or 40 people in the dorms. There were three or four floors in the building; the ground floor was for classes, and the upper floors for sleeping.

The bedrooms were large and square, arranged in semi-circles, with the oldest kids in the back and the little kids in front near the nuns' station. There were always nuns on duty.

My mother visited most weekends.

School was good enough, but I didn't join in regular things for a while. I built traps and cages, for birds and squirrels that I caught in the forest preserves nearby. Someone helped me build cages with two-by-fours and chicken wire. When I caught the squirrels no one told on me. I caught a lot of birds. I was amazed that I could capture them—just a small boy climbing a tree with a homemade cage... Once I climbed a tree and stuck my hand down a hole and caught a red-headed woodpecker. And once I killed a bird with a sling shot. I couldn't believe I had done that—I never used one again.

I got ice skates when I was 10, and I got very good at skating and won some kind of award.

I climbed a lot of trees and fell twice, landing on my back. I remember hunting for hickory nuts in a wooded area. And I went fishing a lot, always alone. I made a rod out of a stick of some kind. No one kept track... I didn't know where everyone else was.

In the summers there was no school and we were able to do pretty much what we wanted. We weren't supposed to leave the grounds, but I did. They could see me coming and going. There were two nuns and you'd get called in and then you'd get a paddle or the strap. I stopped going out the way they could see me, and they didn't know where I was.

I probably missed a lot of meals.

One summer there were a group of young men who came to the school—I think they were training for the priesthood—they were called "yellow jackets" because of the jackets they wore. They played games with us. But other than that, the whole time I was at the school, no adult ever talked with me, ever asked me how I was doing or gave me advice or anything.

I don't remember a soul, not a single name from the training school. Every time I left somewhere it was like a complete blank. My memories are not of people, but of things I did. Some things I did with others, but I have no idea who they were. The younger kids did not befriend each other.

When I was 12, I moved in with my mother and brother and sister, who were all living in my grandmother's house. My mother had a low-level job with the government, and she took the early train into Chicago every day. She had that job for over 20 years. On Saturdays she'd work in the garden. We all went to Mass together on Sunday. There was Sunday breakfast, and Sunday dinner. My mother did the cooking.

I didn't have much interaction with my siblings. I remember going to a movie with my sister when I was 13, the only thing I ever remember doing with her. She also gave me her bike to ride to the golf course. My brother didn't like me. He was told that he would miss his vacation because I was getting into trouble.

I remember my mother favorably. We were close but we couldn't talk. She liked my brother better. She didn't have time for us. She was always working.

I remember getting into a big fight with my uncle—"Francie" was his name, probably for Frank, or Francis. He drank too much and was out of a job. He fed my grandmother cold pea soup and I insisted that no, he *couldn't do that, and I heated up some other food for her. It was a bad fight.*

I pray for him now.

There was a big field near my grandmother's house that they flooded every winter and we played ice hockey out there.

My grandmother had only one eye. She was housebound for years, but rarely did anyone come by to visit. We knew neighbors, and they knew our family—a lot of older Irish families knew my grandfather, Patrick Deering—but my mother had no friends. Somehow no one ever came by. What brought about this distance? I always had a strange feeling about it...

When my grandmother died my mother asked me to call the undertaker. She thanked me later.

In 7th and 8th grade people said I should become a priest. After I got confirmed, before high school, I stopped going to church. I wanted to go to the Catholic high school—for sports. I didn't know what to do. Someone should have said we couldn't afford it, but no one said a thing. I went to the public high school.

Between my sophomore and junior years something just happened and I didn't go back to school in the fall. I was peculiar enough that no one said anything. My mother didn't say anything. The school didn't say anything. I was lost. I didn't know what I was doing.

When I turned 17 I joined the Air Force and was sent to Lackland in Texas. My brother was drafted to Korea and got married when he returned. I didn't go to his wedding; I was in the Air Force. My sister also married when I was away—a Jewish man. We didn't see much of her after that. I don't think she had any children.

In the Air Force I did office work. While I was there I thought of schools to go to. For a while I thought I'd go somewhere and learn to golf professionally. I ended up at Lake Forest College, where my sister had gone. I had my GED, and I told the admissions people I could pass any course, and they let me in. Perhaps they knew of my sister.

I worked a lot while I was in college. I cleaned people's yards. If I saw a pile of dirt I'd knock at the door and ask if I could shovel it. For a while I worked at a private club for wealthy kids, teaching them to ice skate, golf, play baseball. Later, I took a job at a home of 8- to 12-year olds from broken families, taking them on trips to Chicago, to the museums, and to the lake.

My mother told me that she came to my college graduation, but I never saw her. She said she looked for me.

When Jane and I got divorced in 1970 or 72, the lawyers made me say that I'd abandoned her, although the opposite was true. Nobody talked to me about it. But rather than hassle I even paid alimony for a year—then I wrote to her that we should change the arrangement so that we could both get on with our lives.

I didn't go back to Illinois after the divorce, didn't see my mother. I knew that if I went to see her, I'd want to visit Jane, and that would make Jane very angry.

My sister Maryann sent a letter to me at Colorado State in 1976 saying our mother had died. It was addressed very generally, but the college managed to locate me. I was working in the book warehouse then. Somehow I couldn't believe that she had died. I called Maryann—she was living in California—and we talked a while. She gave me information on the whereabouts of my brother, who was still in Illinois and had nine children.

Nine children. Astonishing. But I didn't talk to him until we needed the money for the house in San Francisco.

Here Robert paused a few moments, as if the story were being told to him, too, as he related it to me. There was something tangled up in it that we were not getting to. Then he said, suddenly, "When you're 7 years old and no one tells you anything and it falls on you… and then suddenly you're supposed to go home, and what's that? And then the very next day after you get home you're sent out to caddy at the golf course… I put the golf bag on backwards! No one ever told me what to do. Things just happened to me and I never knew what was going on."

To be left at age 5 and again at 7 is all the leaving that is required to feel abandoned, and in many ways Robert had been lost for most of his young life. Still, listening to him that night in the restaurant, I felt mildly…betrayed. The story he told was similar to the skeletal one I'd imagined all these years, but also fundamentally different. In the little he'd told us, Robert had always portrayed himself as totally on his own. After the institution—"the home", he called it—he had moved back to his grandmother's house with his mother and older brother and sister. I had thought he never saw his mother again, that he was an orphan, but it was his family he returned to, all of them, and the routine of school and sports and Mass and Sunday dinners, whom he now dismissed with a shrug and a shake of his head. They did not seem so horrible. Why had he never allowed them into his life?

I had asked for his story, and now I felt weighed down—not by the story, but by his huge passivity about it. "No one told me a thing," Robert repeated several times. He had been put on his own too early, not talked to, not cared for. And then he had no idea how to talk or be cared-for.

It was late. We were the last people in the restaurant. I saw our server glance at us from where he stood, watching the TV over the bar and waiting for us to finish.

"No one told me a thing, either, Robert," I said suddenly, irritated.

That wasn't true. I had been told plenty; I just hadn't felt loved much. I had learned early to talk and pretend, ask questions and befriend, and then pretend some more until I found what felt like a home. Robert, too, had learned to listen and observe, and ask questions and pretend. But with him there was no talking he could do, no home to be found. Even after all these years, my friendship was not enough to create a home for him. There was really no comparison in our stories, or perhaps even anything similar between us now, really, except this feeling of abandonment and pattern of longing in each of us.

Possible But Not Actual

R ight before we bought the house on De Haro Street, when Kevin was a year and a half old, I saw an ad for a low-residency MFA program at Warren Wilson College, a small liberal arts school in North Carolina. The concept of "low-residency" writing programs was relatively new then, and I was immediately drawn to the idea of living my life and writing at home, working with a writer/mentor one-on-one via mail, and traveling twice a year to North Carolina. It seemed a rightful integration of writing and study into "real" life. John was supportive. Even though we hardly saw Robert, I managed to catch him going out one day and tell him I had been admitted into the program. His face brightened momentarily from its habitual solemnity, and he reached out and put his hand on my arm. "That's wonderful news. That will be very good for you." I began the program in poetry in January of 1986.

Everything about the program and Warren Wilson College was exhilarating to me—the plane ride every six months from San Francisco to Asheville; the funky dorm rooms (cold in January, hot in July) and beautiful rural campus; the faculty (all talented writers and teachers); and the other students (about 70 of them at that time) from all over the country.

Early in each residency, we were to note our preferences for a faculty advisor for the upcoming semester and then be content with whomever we were assigned. A notice would be posted. We had heard about how faculty would negotiate with each other for their roster of three to four students each semester, and everyone wanted badly to be wanted. It was a huge feeding of both soul and ego to be seen, to "be" a writer for 10 days, to talk with others who were as intense as I was about it (and worse), enjoy the readings every night, and get different perspectives on my writing in the workshops, to read others' work closely and learn to articulate a response.

In the daily workshops we tried to pretend we were more humble and less judgmental and comparative than we were. There were classes on form and craft from the visiting and core faculty, as well as graduating students. Faculty readings each night were followed by long conversations in the dorm lounge, or an excursion to the Waffle House for a snack. The two dance parties each residency, with sound system and tapes brought by a student, were a blurry, wonderfully mindless release of energy. Hardly anyone stayed on the sidelines. Students and faculty alike, we all tried to joke and dance our way out of ourselves. In the two years of the program most of us worked very hard on our writing and annotations, and I think most would say the experience of practicing and revising and tossing and talking about it with others was "priceless." In the tiny world of poetry and literary fiction, this felt like the Big Time to me. Egos included, it was a place of kinship for me, where I felt I belonged.

And I welcomed leaving home, exiting my ordinary life, where John was teaching in a private high school in the East Bay and I worked as a typesetter four days a week at *PC World Magazine*—enough for health benefits. In the morning I would pick up a co-worker, drop Kevin off at daycare, and drive downtown to my job. On the side I also did occasional word processing, typing doctoral theses, former professors' book manuscripts, and other random projects, cultivating an outlier's pride in being the hired help for others' projects, imagining that someday those whose manuscripts I was typing would say, "Oh, I knew her!" Motivated by my "free day to write" and the ongoing connection with my advisor, I was very happy. Like before college in Colorado, I felt in the midst of potential.

At 27, I was one of the youngest students in the program. I remember there was talk in the administration about not admitting students who were too young, who hadn't had enough in-the-world experience to process either success or failure—never mind the intensity of the work itself and the charged atmosphere of being with all the other writers, each bringing their soul's work and needs and driving egos into the mix.

Like many, I thrived on the flashflood flirtations with students and faculty—in the writing, the dinners, the dances, and the long letters during the semester. I felt recognized; I acted independent; I wrote with a sharp edge; "needy" would never be a word to describe me, and yet I was quite needy. The flirtations became content for the writing. I had become good at looking over my shoulder to see who was looking.

Students and Teachers

> *"A snowflake is not always octagonal. Pay attention to facts."*

In the bar I found I knew
your ex-wife's writing,

though I didn't know
she was your ex-wife.
"That man she was getting
away from
in those highway poems?
That was me."
We had another scotch.

Neither of us mentioned
our lovers, you awaiting
an invitation and me wondering
where approval left off
and desire began. And if
that nervous embrace in the hallway
had leapt to our mouths, if
our bedtime talk had been
face to close face instead
of through the thin studio wall
of my apartment, what
would we know better?

In the morning you shuffled
to the bathroom, made a joke
about the red birthmark on your chest--
your "map of France," you called it--
and I imagined how you must have said that
to surprised lovers,
only at night, in dimness,
instead of morning.

You took a shower, looked at a poem
of mine, smoked a cigarette
in that hideous gold chair by the window.

Listen to the music underneath
your poem, you said,
don't correct all your errors
before you make them.

That afternoon you left
with a dark-haired woman
who filled the room around you
with adoration.
She was a nice woman, also
a student, though perhaps not
as attractive or attentive
as myself. (I tended to tally.)
I had a grilled cheese sandwich,
called my boyfriend,
pondered what you said.

Oh who are teachers
without students? What lovers
without writing in between?
I have corrected all my errors
and made none. What opportunity
have I missed? Bring back
that map. I'll put
my hands on that map.

At our last session at Warren Wilson, the graduating MFA
class received, finally, a brief talk on the mechanics and
possibilities for publication. This talk was wisely saved until the
very end to try and help keep us students focused on the work
at hand during the program, rather than how to find readers.
The faculty facilitating the talk surely knew that very few in the
room would continue writing, never mind publish anything. I

suppose there was no way to say that to us—at that point it would have been like saying, "Most of you will die. A few will survive." They did not know, really, who might go on to be successful. (And many in that room eventually did publish and go on to be good teachers and editors themselves.)

What is community, and how is it to be found? For many of us, Warren Wilson was not just an innovative school of talented writers. It was "church" in some way, a place to be known and supported and loved. The drive to work on and share our writing was genuine and deep, but it was also necessarily fed by our individual egos and aspirations.

Still, I did think I would be one of the lucky ones. I had been affirmed, and I was full of potential—possibility but not actuality. You can live in potential for a long time; it can become a habit.

Connecticut
1988 - 1992

B efore I finished the MFA, we moved to the east coast, into the house in Connecticut where John had grown up and his father still lived. It was supposed to be temporary, just for a year, an opportunity for a change. We had told Robert of our plans and made arrangements with my sister and her friend to move into the house on De Haro Street and pay our share of the mortgage. It was hard to tell what Robert thought or how he felt; he had been mostly incognito downstairs for the three years since we had bought the house, leaving early and returning late. If I needed to communicate, I left a note on his door like I used to do in Colorado. My anger over this covered a sadness I was tired of. I would be relieved to be away from him and the city for a year.

A few days before we left I heard the jangle of his keys one night outside the door and stepped out to say goodbye. "We'll be leaving Friday," I said. "We're almost packed up." In the dark I couldn't see his face clearly at the bottom of the short stairway leading to his door, but it was apparent he wasn't coming up for a goodbye hug.

"Is there anything you need me to do?" he asked.

"No, I think we're all set."

"Well, have a safe trip," he said, as if we were distant housemates and nothing more.

"Thank you, we will." I couldn't wait to get out of town.

John's father Ed had emphysema and needed assistance, and John's siblings were very glad when we arrived in Connecticut. They made us feel welcome, using their portion of an aunt's inheritance to build another bathroom in the house so that Ed could move downstairs. John got a job teaching high school in Bridgeport, and for a few months I did not have to work. Three of John's siblings lived nearby and visited often, bringing dinner and hanging out with us. They took care of us. I had never experienced family that way, in an easy back and forth, with relaxed expressions of affection and few expectations. So this was how John, as the youngest, had been surrounded and encouraged.

It was a sweet time. Life was much easier on a dead-end street in the Connecticut suburbs than it was in San Francisco. In the mornings after Kevin went to kindergarten, I would take Ed to the senior center, work for a few hours on short stories for my master's thesis, meet Kevin at the bus stop in the afternoon, and make dinner. There was an ease, breathing room, less struggle. Instead of being escorted to the park, Kevin went straight outside without asking permission. He learned to ride a bike; he climbed all the trees and the street signs, too. Other boys came over and they shot baskets in the hoop across the street and constructed forts under blankets in his bedroom. Unlike San Francisco, the summer was hot; windows were left open, and sometimes the air was completely still and quiet. After 10 years in the city, I felt at home in Connecticut.

I wondered what kind of a job I should try and get. Should I try to find a job at a college teaching composition, a common path for a poet or fiction writer, with hopes of eventually getting a full-time position?

"When I teach undergraduates, I always feel that I'm in a nest of baby birds, all screaming for a worm," one faculty member at Warren Wilson said to me. "Don't be a teacher unless you like to teach." It was worthy advice; I knew I was not a teacher. I worried there would be no energy left for anything else. Could I find a way to just work part-time my whole life, sacrificing security for that open writing time?

But the fact was I did not know, really, how to use that time. I did know that a writer's life would always be marginal and parsed and exhausting. I was at an impasse, tired of comparing and longing, tired of sending packets of poems and stories out to publications and getting them back with strange little notes *("Your stories have many nice things in them..." "My reluctance about each is different..." "The story finally seems too <u>cruel</u>, to me, anyway..." "I hope you'll send us more work to consider..."),* and sending them back out again. If I were published, what would it mean, anyway? It did not take too much imagination to see that publishing a book did not, for most, change your life by providing income or employment opportunities.

I had worn myself out with waiting and wanting. The idea of Being a Writer and the need for recognition had overwhelmed the desire to actually (I won't say "simply") write. How long it has taken me to see the need for attention underneath this pattern, imprinted during those long talks with Robert, in which almost anything could be and was said.

And, of course, understanding a need does not necessarily make it go away. Untangling the desire for attention from the desire to just write, "without hope or expectation," as it is said, is a writer's ongoing cross. In the satiation of ordinary lived life, sometimes that desire fades into silence. That's the risk—maybe the blessing.

When would the sense of "potential" just be the present tense: my life, writing or not, right then, as it was? I suddenly wanted to have another baby, and I wanted this second child with my whole body—with complete, frightening, fulfilling abandon.

My mind-self saw the desire as sabotage, diversion. I knew this choice would shut down many possibilities, especially the availability of time, but from somewhere deeper I needed a plainer self. It was not that straightforward, of course; it only looks that way now.

When Ed died peacefully in his sleep a year and a half after we moved to Connecticut, John's siblings were happy to have us stay in the house. We were immersed in our lives, John teaching, Kevin in school. I got a part-time job in the Development Department at a local university, a position I knew I could keep when I became pregnant.

In the winter of 1992, a few months after our daughter Clara was born, Robert came to visit us for the first time since we had moved east. The video distribution business where he had been working for the past few years had gone bankrupt and he was unemployed again. He came for a couple of weeks, and the visit was an interlude, with breathing room for all of us. In the morning, after John and Kevin had gone off to school, Robert took care of the baby while I made breakfast. I picture him with Clara on his shoulder, talking to her, humming a little song, looking out the window at the snow in the backyard. Had I ever heard him hum before? In the afternoons John came home, and I went to my job.

Robert's visit was filled with normal, day-to-day things and not so much talk of the kind we had done before. This was the first time he spoke at length of his childhood, of when his mother left him at the training school, of wandering in the woods near the "home," of playing football in high school. I asked him about what happened when we were living upstairs from him on De Haro Street. He said he didn't know, exactly, something about knowing it would, again, not be a home for him. He said everything had changed between us—I had my own family now—and he feared being too close and then losing everything, as usual.

This rare straightforwardness drew me in; it made me think of the tormented letters we exchanged in 1981 when we decided not to see each other for those few months. When Robert flew back to San Francisco, I wrote him several letters.

February 1992

Your visit was so nice for us because we all had some breathing room. That's the way I'd like it for us from now on. It was filled with normal, day-to-day things, and not endless analysis, endless editing. Those things are more important than lifetimes of critical thinking.

So what are you going to do with yourself? Have I said what I feel? If this house thing pulls through, or even if it doesn't, I'd like you to come east. Stay with us a while. (John even considered asking you to live with us, but that would be more intimacy than I can handle.) See how quickly I get hopeful? How much hope can I afford, I ask myself. When you moved into De Haro with us, I was hoping for that kind of neighbor thing, that dropping in, that ease that comes from knowing you'll see plenty of the people you love, so you don't cling so hard to them. You have them in your daily life. But that didn't happen. You went down. When I think of that I feel again reluctant.

I don't have any control over you going down. But the fear of that makes me necessarily distant.

Of course you understand all this.

This is what I guess I want response to, with regard to your future plans. I've enclosed the details about the house, and of course we will talk about all

the practicalities. But I am asking, again, for
something from you. I want some talk from you.
There are two beautiful cardinals right outside
my window right now. Perfect and red.

Robert did not respond to my letters; instead, we spoke
frequently on the phone. He was in a bad place. His
unemployment had run out; he still had no job; and he couldn't
pay his share of the mortgage or taxes. He cursed the
unemployment offices and the inconsiderate people on public
transportation. He explained to me in detail why the garbage
bill would be higher this time around, what the heating bill
would be, what his income for last year was. Like an old man,
he explained. I sat there in our living room in Connecticut,
watching the baby try and strangle herself with the phone cord,
wishing he would stop talking. I felt guilty for the amounts I
had recently charged on our credit card, knowing that my
friend was broke.

"It's a mess I'm in," he would say, or, sometimes, "It's a
mess I've gotten myself into." After a while that only made me
angry because we did not know what to do for him. I extended
my boring job at the university to full-time as we took on
Robert's share of the mortgage for a while. I knew he was
ashamed about us having to do that; I told him I considered
these payments reimbursement for the loans he had given us
on the house and for my word processing business. As the
months went on and his situation became more dire, and it
became clearer that we would be staying in Connecticut, we
finally decided to sell the house. It was a bad time for real estate
and the house remained on the market for a long time.

September

Dear Virginia,

...About the house: you are right to say that, for me, the house is becoming an albatross; so both the long and short term solution for me is to sell it as soon as possible. And yes I felt guilty because I cannot help. And yes I want to apologize. That I feel responsible is something I cannot change.

...Thanks for avoiding what could be hurtful. We sometimes have the wrong ideas about persons; we think that like computers they can be re-booted and something entirely new will come out: bum one day, hero the next. Well a boot won't change who I am after all these years. But I still hope. We have an obligation to hope as long as we're alive, perhaps especially when everything seems hopeless. Stay a friend as long as you can.

Love, Robert

At the end of the year, the house finally sold, at the bottom of the market. John and I didn't care that we did not get much from the sale, figuring we had lived there; we had loved that house. Robert found another apartment by Golden Gate Park and a job at a bookstore in downtown San Francisco. It had been a hard year and we were relieved it was over.

We're Not Dead Yet, Are We?
Two Letters
1993

July

Virginia,
    Thank you for the cards and photos and letters,
which I always enjoy very much—they always move me
to remembering and ruminating and smiling to
myself—but they disturb my complacent (I'd say smug,
but it suggests a self satisfaction which I never feel—
have no reason to feel) pointless disappearing act.
Communication is like a cat appearing suddenly
outside your window. Thick furred silver-gray
apparition creeping down a stairway, long tail in a
straight line as if it were hunting. Hunting what? A
maybe; a perhaps; an imaginary anything; a possible
something hides just there. Or there! This cat is almost
irresistible; plays around, preys around, shows up at
odd hours, freezes you for long moments.
    I'm taking a week off from work this week, the first
time since I've worked at the bookstore. I have been
for several months a floor supervisor, which I had
previously resisted, since you lose your union
membership and the health benefits that go with
them; and you take on a good deal more stress from

problem resolution, etc, etc. The pay is greater, of course, and with it I am just able to pay the absurdly high rent for my apartment and the utilities etc...

In one photograph, you're standing with the mirror behind you, I see your mother in a way I hadn't noticed till now. A season you can't notice from a distance. In my dreams you are always much younger, as much a product of memory as of invention. It seems curious in a way that I have no dreams about the (a) future—no dream for a future either; never had that, another kind of failure I can't explain but carry around. Memory is wedded to the past naturally and logically, of course, but as I age memory seems to dominate over invention, as if I were falling backwards, I suppose.

My vacation has brought me to Tassahara on Cole St., which I get to rarely now. A good place to visit: Here is a woman with two brownies, one chocolate, one butterscotch; and two squares of cake, one with white frosting, carrot cake probably, and one square of chocolate, frosting the same. One square and one brownie disappear so fast I wonder if it is without tasting them, her fork a miniature backhoe over the moist ground of cake.

She wears 6 multicolored, beaded bracelets on her right hand, three on her left, our cake excavator. She has on washed-out mustard shorts, an extra large sweatsuit gray t-shirt, tri-colored tennis shoes, a blue-rose-purple combo—Haight St. for sure, upper I'd guess—on the chair beside her are two large bags, one cotton blue and white stripes, the other plastic, flamingo pink. Filled with? I don't know. If not a denizen, she is at least a neighborhood necessity in Cole Valley. Except for her age—she is in her early 40's

I think—she might be an afternoon tea match for Mr. Hilditch. As she works through the last bit of cake, she exhibits a mastery of one rhythm method for sensual pleasure.

Mr. Hilditch is a principal in Felicia's Journey, *William Trevor's latest work. It is a very good book, almost a great one. When you come out in August bring along an extra suitcase for books.*

Scribbled on the bathroom wall in Tart To Tart, near Eighth and Irving, close to where I live: "GO UNABOMBER". This is crossed out, and, beneath it, in RED marker is "STUPID," then, below this, again, "GO UNABOMBER." Do you miss the city?

Everywhere you go now it is like this. It's not the bizarre that frightens us, nor the sudden violence next door, nor are we once again being reminded how temporal we are, how temporal and changeable everything is: It's not the economy, it's the utter stupidity of the failure to face... Well enough of that.

The city is where I have to stay in order to find a decent job until I'm 70, if I make it that far. And there are benefits: Good Coffee, Fresh corn and peaches which I buy at a market at 22nd & Irving, and granny smiths. And we have leg days, summer brown legs in light summer dresses. Such, along with what reading I'm able to do are my entertainments.

My truck runs, though I never use it; I had to get a battery a month ago because the old one died for lack of use. And, of course, no movies or books or people. But I'm still addicted to books and ideas. It's absurd the way I buy books, but the fact of them, the material presence of them, the anticipated touch and use of them is my (imagined?) link with—with what? I really hope to look at them someday.

The ostensible reason for my Vacation is to read: the reading is varied; some poetry, some stories. I enjoy the work of it, and the solitude (cutting myself off from everything and being alone is not the same as solitude)... There are many things I would like to have the time for, but my work days are often very long now and I find it very difficult to work at something when I get home. I also procrastinate, and I love to muse, neither of which helps to accomplish anything. At one time I hoped that I would find something, anything; and a kind of talent to go with it and then maybe to work at it and do something, but I never did—never have and with a very ordinary mind and a lot of insecurities & fears I am—Well for now I am the Imperial Potentate of Payroll who decides whether you have worked 8 hrs or only 7.56 or perhaps have worked 8 hrs and will be paid .50 (1/2 hour) overtime. The overtime will help to buy books and so feed my silly addiction. Voila! C'est un Balance!

The fog was so thick last night when I took my walk that my jacket was soaked when I came home, and this morning, early—because it's street sweeping day and I must move the truck—the trees and bushes were soaked and dripping. End of heat wave.

I do miss you, and think of you all often even though I never write. I hope you'll save me at least a morning or an afternoon when you come out. I will try to get a few days off... and perhaps we can work something out.

I do not talk to anyone at work, though we talk
about work and on the off days I only speak to say
"Coffee, please," but I'll remember how once we start.
And so on.

Love, Robert

September

Dear Robert,

Yesterday was Kevin's 10th birthday. He'd said the night before that tomorrow would be the best day of his life. I tried to talk him down. ...Ah, the pleasures and tensions of suburban living.

John worked much of the summer converting half of the garage into a new office for us.

We've acquired two kittens—Annie and Carlisle (for Kitty Carlisle, of course). Carlisle is a dusty orange male. He's sleek and strong and laid back (the only cat I've ever seen who can sleep on his back with one paw straight up in the air). Annie, his sister who was lost for a couple days after birth (and named for the Orphan by the woman who gave us the cats) is a spotted calico-like cat—not as strong or friendly, but smart. They adore each other, and play for three hours, then sleep. I am very glad we got two together. The kids each have their own way of enjoying the cats (Carlisle will even tolerate an occasional vigorous hug from Miss Clara; Kevin torments them, but takes care of the litter box). Even John likes them.

I'm getting very flippant here, but I am basically happy. In fact, this life right this minute seems so close to everything I would ever want that I get frightened. It seems dangerous to be in your life and not full of hopeless longing...

I have been reading the Wm. Trevor you sent— what great stories; I love their complete sentences. I also bought the first book of poetry I've bought in a long time: Mary Oliver. Very non-experimental and refreshing. Perhaps too ecstatic for me, but, then, I only read a few a day. Some of the poems make me think of you, of the way you think of animals and the way it seems to me you have striven to be generous with everyone but yourself....

In all my errand-running and cleaning and arranging of the past few weeks, I cleaned out the basement, finally going through some of the boxes from De Haro that had been sitting down there for a year. I came upon the box marked "COLLEGE NOTEBOOKS" and threw most of them out. What use are they to me? Everything has to be read again and again. I'm no Cliff Notes. One notebook, however, was from your class, Intro To Philosophy. It was strange and tender and embarrassing to read my notes, which were really a dialogue with you. Mr. Bullshit, I called you on pg. 1. Apparently at some point I gave you the notebook to read, and you wrote comments in it. (Of course I would forget all this, of course.) How excited I was to be in college; how I was in love with myself through you; how sad I was to have lost my family. I probably shouldn't even write this from "perspective"—it's like trying to pretend I didn't feel the way I did.

At one point in the notebook I was writing definitions for some reason: "love - a deep or tender feeling of affection for a person or persons" —and following that is your first comment:

"Persons are not objects. No doubt there is a trunk somewhere waiting to bear the weight of us— we who will be discarded, affectionately, like no longer useful toys. And will you dig me out some moving-day; and smile?"

I did dig you out, didn't I (not smiling, though— more with a look of incredulousness). And did I discard you? Have I? How frightened I was, I remember, and attracted. I was attracted to my fear through you, also.

On the following page you write: "Why do you ask questions that cannot be answered by oneself?" Well.

Well, we're not dead yet, are we?

Now I'm going to pick up my two-year-old. We would all like for you to visit; you'd love that path we took when you last came—all the leaves changing.

I was right in my letter—I did dig Robert out. Even as he was taking care of me when I first came to college, I was learning how to reach in and dig him out of himself. In revealing myself, I was hoping to reveal him, as if in that revelation we would somehow both be safe, and enough. I thought I could change him or at least help him change or find help. Over many years it had become a way of being with him.

The "Christian Thing to Do"

February 7, 1999

Dear R—

Many happy returns of the day…. You probably do not even remember the day when it's your birthday.

There's much to tell, and yet not much at all… the biggest thing being that I will probably become confirmed as a Catholic at Easter. The thing itself is not such a big deal—it seems like a natural evolution… remember *The Sound of Music*?… I always wanted to be a Catholic. Have wanted some ritual that is larger and more consistent than our family rituals. "What if we get a divorce over this?" I ask John, and he says, "Oh, Virginia, you're just doing the kind of work you've always done." It is work, thinking about God. Anyhow, telling people about it. So mostly I don't talk about it.

There's more to the story, but that will have to be in person.

I joined the Catholic Church. Or, I should say, I joined St. James, which is Catholic. A friend brought me to that parish, advocating "participation," appreciating the purple, dark, waiting time of Advent and the familiarity of the communion ritual, the same all over the world. Rev. Thomas Lynch, the pastor of St. James, sealed the deal by making the joining seem like a natural step for me, a following-through.

"It's simple," he said. "You've had a spiritual life for a long time, probably, through your writing. You want a place to root it." That a priest saw so clearly that writing could be a spiritual seeking was the encouragement I needed.

I was not completely "unchurched." As a girl, I had talked to God quite a lot. Written him letters, in fact. "Dear God," my journal entries begin when I was 10, striking up a conversation with God that evolved. I was an early adolescent, having a hard time at school in our latest new home in Irving, Texas. When I told my mother that I wanted to go to church, she looked through the phone book then dropped me off at the local Episcopal church. I was immediately attracted to the ritual and "common prayer." A couple of months later, she started attending, dragging along my brother and sisters. Then, to keep an eye on my mother, Dad joined, too. The following year we were all baptized at the same service.

Once prompted, the longing to belong to something bigger resurfaced. At St. James, I was drawn to the Mass each week, to the old institution and its beautiful, repetitive ritual and messy variety of people. St. James was diverse. I would watch the communion procession—old, young, many ethnicities, many poor, a few well-off. I knew for certain that I did not believe in the same way as many of them, and yet there we were together, piety and hypocrisy, searching and accepting of others (at least for the moment), and I was among them, whichever "I" was present that day. Somehow this moved me then and continues to move me now, after many years. Although some years I have belonged more than others, I know that the practice of church helps to take me from being an individual to being a person, where I am more free.

I craved Eucharist, the coming-together, the bread and wine, food and offering between disparate souls. "It's simple," Fr. Tom said, again, although I suspected it might not be so. "It's love. You're craving love." I must have looked perplexed. "It's not a head thing, Virginia. You won't get to it through thinking."

I felt bashful about revealing my newfound joining to my family and writer friends, but those who knew me understood. As Fr. Tom had said, the desire to join came from a different knowing than reason or intellect.

John, raised Catholic, quietly started coming to Mass with me. In our conversations, we had found a new place to be together. After 16 years of civil marriage, we bought wedding rings, and invited his nearby family to witness a wedding ceremony the week before I was confirmed. Clara, now 7, was baptized while Kevin witnessed in pagan teenage amusement.

What would Robert think? I was nervous. On my annual visit to California I told him about the upcoming confirmation. As though the church was a new lover, I described to him Eucharist and the feeling of belonging. Maybe through church I could re-become myself. It sounded good as I said it.

Robert listened with interest but seemed unsurprised. "It's good you're joining the church," he said. After a long pause he added, "I was raised Catholic," he said. "The home was Catholic. Back when it was all in Latin."

Why did I not know this? Like the existence of his brother, he had not yet told me his story, only bits and pieces.

April 1999

Dear Robert,

...As of Saturday night, I'm signed, sealed and delivered into the Catholic Church... Anyhow, what I didn't say in my last note to you was how I'd forgotten how much alike we are. We always have been. We see the world so similarly that it's eerie. I'd forgotten that, until we started talking in that café about religion.... This is aside from your particular skill (sometimes it's a trick) at making everyone feel most themself... It's a "confirming" thing, to know someone who, way down, past circumstance, peeled-away, is the way you are and, mostly, often, feels the way you do. When I was younger, I knew this and felt this—the potential power and danger of it, and shied away, made it into a kind of mystical connection. I did and did not want you to be in love with me. I had no place for that love. Perhaps (of course) there were parental connections—but aren't parental connections supposed to feel that way at their best?... Then later I tried to domesticate the feeling, incorporate it, struggled (mostly in vain) to know "you". And now for many years you haven't been in my life in any way at all.

I'm not sure what I'm getting at. There's no conclusion to the observation. I am grateful that you're still alive, literally, and feel sad that we don't participate more in each other's lives. You don't want to be a burden to me, I know, and I don't want you to be one. However and nevertheless, people are these things to each other whether they're together or apart. I had a stunning dream last week in which I said to you something like, "Well, I may as well know you while you're alive." I then said I'd talk to John and see about you moving in with us. I suppose that is a conclusion of a sort.

You really should be in our lives. Starting with a visit very soon. There's not all that much time on this earth. (Do I sound Converted? Do I sound Saved? Forgive me!)

It was four and a half years later before we invited Robert to come permanently to the East Coast. Though we didn't speak directly of it, the offer was made and accepted knowing the urgency of his decompensation. There was an obligation, even if I did not want to acknowledge it as such. He was familial, part of my family—odd uncle, askew father—and I the partial, reluctant daughter. Both of us had ruptures in our family relationships and did not know how to perform our roles well. When I went to San Francisco to get him, I didn't think much about it. I did not go because it was "the Christian thing to do," as someone at St. James suggested. Any thoughts I had were positive, exuberant, naïve, maybe even manic. I did not think, *I will save him,* although maybe I thought he could be saved.

Part II

Nine Months

2004

Robert settled in with us in Connecticut. The winter was not cruel, the cold not as cold as it could have been. I made up the small bedroom for him, with a new twin bed, a dresser and two bookcases. He used the downstairs bathroom, so we all had some privacy. I bought him a yoga mat and a fleece bathrobe, which he wore like a sweater all day so he didn't "catch a chill," along with the same sweat pants and sweatshirt more days in a row than I would have liked. He listened carefully as I showed him how to load the washer. Each week, just a small pile of laundry: four pairs of socks, cargo pants, a T-shirt so threadbare it seemed made of silk, and the same two pairs of boxers.

He was fit, but very thin. One day he said, "I looked in the mirror and realized I looked like I just came out of a concentration camp."

The exuberance we had felt at exiting San Francisco faded quickly. Every morning he was at the kitchen table. Up before us, he had made the coffee, always too weak in spite of our instructions. I always wanted to throw it out and start over, but instead I would pour a quarter-cup and drink it, politely. "Good morning," one or the other of us always said, and the other responded, "Good morning."

Our politeness covered an abyss. If Robert was in a good mood (and sensed I was in a good mood, too), he would slide the folded newspaper across the table toward me—a book review, a poet's obituary, an article about warblers. Since I like mornings to myself, I tried to be patient. I told myself it is hard to live with anyone. I sat on the step by the back door, put on my socks and shoes and headed out for a walk. When I returned in half an hour he would be in the same place, but by then John or Clara were usually at the table, too, having breakfast before going off to work and school.

Sometimes he stopped reading the paper and stared at us, rubbing his beard, taking us in. We pretended not to notice.

He wanted to pay us rent. We declined, so instead Robert bought us wine and coffee, and cleaned the kitchen. We would leave the room and let him do it his way, thoroughly, with too much soap and the annoying squeal of the hot water pipe going on and off, on and off.

Evenings were better than mornings. We ate many good meals together with the wine that he bought, taking our time, conversing for a couple of hours about politics, baseball, our work, people at church. There was a thread of lovingkindness through these evenings.

As the days went on with him living in our house, I felt Robert's dependence on me and love like a child's—a palpable and longing presence. He seemed content here in Connecticut, like he was when he first moved to San Francisco. Why wouldn't I want that for him? Yet sometimes I felt like he was sucking my own happiness in this place from me, as though there was not enough happiness to go around. It was…ridiculous, and I knew he would be dismayed to know I was feeling this way.

After a few weeks, we made an agreement that he would go out in the morning so I could have the house to myself before I left for work, an ironic arrangement, since he would go to the coffeehouse nearby where I stopped most mornings to get my coffee. So there he was, again. I did not acknowledge him, and he conveniently placed himself at a table behind a display rack so I wouldn't have to.

Had it been like this when Robert stayed with my sister and me, back in San Francisco? When I brought him here, I had not thought through the details of how our daily lives in the same house would unfold. Perhaps I thought he would only be with us a very short while before he found his own place. He had needed rescue and we rescued him, but we never talked about that time, as though the apartment with the windows covered in black plastic bags had never existed.

The 30 boxes we had shipped from California finally arrived, and John helped him stack them carefully in our garage. He retrieved some clothes from the boxes to wear to church—a new, too-small, button-down shirt and high-waisted slacks— all clean. At church I glanced sideways at him, taking in the thinning, beautiful white hair and the tips of his large ears, like a 71-year-old boy.

Robert came to St. James with us each Sunday, merging alongside us at Mass as though the past 50 years since he had attended were a blip. "It's been a long time," he said. I watched him gently tap his fist against his chest in the old way at the Confiteor (confession) near the beginning of mass: *Mea culpa, mea maxima culpa*—through my fault, through my most grievous fault… This Robert was a stranger to me. Just as I looked at him furtively, sideways, he and I were in a side-by-side relationship with God. We didn't talk about God, or Jesus, or what being a Christian meant to either of us. Somehow it was not in our language, or perhaps even then it was too late in his illness for the talk to take root. Still, I would have liked to have talked to Robert about it all, God and church, when he could still understand.

Then spring was in the air, warming, breaking open. Each day after reading the paper, Robert took a long walk, sometimes eight miles or more, his red shirt tied around his waist. When he was feeling good, we heard all about these walks—elaborate, detailed descriptions of the direction he went and everything he saw along the way in a slow, I-will-not-be-hurried manner. He was authoritative about the location of a certain coreopsis bush, and the mayapple plants, or two herons. He talked about all of his sightings as though he had lived here all his life, as though it was in some way his place and we were the visitors.

He often walked in the woods nearby. "The other day I saw three deer, and they saw me," he said one day in his deliberate way. "They didn't move. We stood looking at each other for a few moments. Then," he paused dramatically, "I leaned over to a branch that was near my head and nipped off a leaf with my mouth. They watched me for a moment and then they stopped watching and went back to what they were doing. I made my way slowly toward them, pausing to paw the ground and to sniff, like they do. I got very close to them."

John and I were quiet. "Well! I wonder what they thought of you!" I said, finally.

When Robert was not in a good place, the walks were longer and he went straight up to his room afterward.

One day he said, "The chickadees are out. I swear I heard them on my walk yesterday." Then he changed the subject abruptly and looked at me intently. "Last night I thought I heard you call out my name."

"Nope." I was learning to keep my responses as casual as possible, as though that would help dismiss the voices he was hearing.

He frowned. "I must have been dreaming. I listened for a while but didn't hear anything else."

I was having my own dreams. In one, I was in church with Robert. It was very crowded. He was in a strange mood; I felt it. Suddenly he started pounding with his palm on the back of the pew in front of us, rocking slightly side to side. He was moaning a little, looking down. At first I wondered whether he had entered some sort of religious ecstasy. People were beginning to turn and look at him. I ran my hand down his back, patting him. When I saw his face I realized it wasn't ecstasy—it was a breakdown. He was crying, falling apart.

Kevin was now at college in Boston, and Clara was in eighth grade. We had told Clara that Robert would be coming to stay with us for a while. She knew him from our visits to San Francisco, his gift to her of a stuffed orange cat that she carried with her everywhere for a while, and the full set of hardbound Beatrix Potter that we had read together until she was 6 or 7. She was used to visitors, and Robert fit well enough into a hybrid category between friends and family that she seemed ready to tolerate if not enjoy.

After Robert had been living with us for three months, we asked Clara how she was feeling about it. With 13-year old candor, she said she was embarrassed by five things, not necessarily in order:

o that she had to introduce him to her friends who came over, and they got weirded-out when she explained he was my "mom's-teacher-from-college" and he was living with us;

o that Robert did exercises in the living room—particularly the arm-swinging ones—right in full view of the living room windows where people might see: "Why can't he do them in his room?";

o that sometimes she came home from school and he was shirtless and washing himself in the kitchen sink, instead of taking a shower: "It would be different if he was all buff and everything, but he's an old man";

o that he always wore the same clothes: blue sweatpants with that T-shirt tucked into his boxers which were sticking out of the sweats, and those weird suspenders holding up everything…

o that he was "so quiet, but always around."

Sometimes he would look across the kitchen table at me like the old days with intense love, like a lover—a full, open, sexual look, knowing and longing all at the same time. I felt it like a challenge: see how strongly I feel for you; see how openly I gaze on you. When I first met him, even though I avoided it, I wanted to be the recipient of that look. But not anymore. I broke the gaze, made a joke. I didn't take the look full-on, for fear he would append himself to me in such a way that I'd never get my life back, that he would carry me down.

Why couldn't I just say, "Don't look at me like that?"

I was afraid of hurting him. Every time I said something straightforward about the situation, something critical or frustrated, he went down. As spring came on, we saw the cycle up close, once or twice a month, where he stayed dramatically out of the way, going out early and coming home late, saying only a quiet, polite, bare minimum.

When John confronted him about this, Robert said it was just not in him to connect with others the way we wanted him to—not enough to find a good living situation or a job. He was intensely alone, he said; it was in him, and there was nothing to be done about it. He tried to explain this a few times. "I see nature as it is," he said one evening. His tone was solemn, as though he were composing a homily. "I watch the swans preening, every day. They can't see themselves in the water, but I can see them—I'm different from them. The geese, looking for food, pecking, but there's no food, nothing there..." He drifted for a moment, then came back. "But they have no anxiety or disappointment about it. When they don't get what they're after they just go on—they don't reflect, they just go on..." He paused again and said, quite formally, "I live in my humanity, in my examination of them. I live in sadness."

He nodded at us, satisfied.

The weeks went by without movement toward a job or apartment, and Robert began to sense our impatience. With John's help, he had bought a used car at a repair shop nearby, which gave all of us more freedom. In a conversation with him one afternoon, John discovered that he was planning for the worst contingency—living from his car. He was considering where he might go that would be cheaper, perhaps south. The concerns he expressed to John were related to the details— how to handle his mail, whether he had clothes that were warm enough.

John was detached; he didn't get angry-into-silence like I did. He could usually make Robert feel better, with patience and talk that was gentle. Why are you spending your energy on the most negative possibility, he asked him, rather than working toward the more positive things? John got him to agree that he was probably clinically depressed (more acceptable to all of us than "delusional disorder," which we somehow knew not to bring up), exhibited and exacerbated by not sleeping, that there was a pattern to it and he needed help.

We asked around and got the names of five psychotherapists and Robert made an appointment with one.

We decided we would continue to follow the plan we had talked about: write an ad to find a place to live; place the ad in the paper and the church bulletin; sign up for senior housing in town; inquire about companion or live-in work. We would follow-up on leads that others had mentioned; we would see what happened.

Would it all be obliterated in a few months, I wondered, when Robert moved away to live in his car? If that happened, it would be his way of punishing both himself and us.

Every morning: John, Robert, and me at the kitchen table. The blue T-shirt, the blue sweats, the white tube socks, the sneakers.

Summer.

I was sitting in the grass between the garden boxes picking the overripe cherry tomatoes. There were hundreds of the beauties, branches swarming in a tangled mess over the grass. Fruit flies hovered and dispersed as I reached in and picked.

"They're all over on the other side," Robert said, from behind the screen door. "Just all over." The tone of his voice implied, *What a waste. You should have let me pick them.*

"Yes, they are," I said. I was a lazy gardener. As I picked the tomatoes, I was acutely aware of him, as I imagined he was of me.

Later he said how he longed to pull the weeds that were creeping into the blank spot where the lettuce got too hot— "the crab grass is taking over"—but that he wouldn't touch it because he remembered I told him not to, back when. I had already watched him weed the gravel driveway, compulsively. I didn't want him working in the garden. It would become like the dishes for him, and in a few weeks it would take all his time, and it would be his.

I knew he wasn't trying to take over our lives. More than anything during those months, perhaps, Robert wanted me to need him, and I refused. It might have been very healing for him if I had asked him to do things and let him find a place with us. But the more he wanted me to need him, the more I refused, and in refusing I began to feel like I was taking everything away from him. I had gotten used to things going wrong for Robert; I could hardly imagine them going right. Some days I wasn't even sure I really wanted them to go right.

I wondered, do all of us, secretly or not-so-secretly, feel a kind of reprieve when things go wrong for others, even those we love? A sort of I-told-you-so mentality, even if nothing was told? Or a Glad-it's-not-me that is so basic and primal to us that we can't resist its relief. As if something went really right for the person, we'd be left out, no longer needed as someone to feel pity for them.

I think of people I love and the way that feels, sensing the webs of their relationships with others—parents and siblings, spouse, former lovers, other friends—all those connections that they bring into their relationship with me. I intuit their individual desires and egos; I see their quirks; sometimes I can see my own quirks in response. I feel frustrated, then engaged. I imagine their lives without me and feel jealous and a bit lonely when I see that they are whole and separate. I want the best for them, but rarely do I want that as much as I want the best for myself. It is not often that am I free enough to be aside and beyond myself enough to want that, to see the person of them.

I knew this was the embarrassing sin, the shackle to be struggled against—the binding-up and stashing-away of love, saving it up as if you'd someday have enough for yourself so that you could freely give the "extra" to others. To really, really wish someone well, and to sacrifice to make it so is love, *love*, I said to myself, aware that I was withholding that from Robert like a resentful child, and feeling powerless to stop.

What I wanted from him he could not seem to give: a real self to push up against, not this shadow of a person. I knew he felt guilty about that; he was used to feeling guilty and clung to the feeling, which only made everything worse.

He went twice to the psychotherapist, then quietly stopped.

"I thought you should know that they're here," he said carefully one evening after dinner. "They must have followed me out here. There are at least five of them. They wear baseball hats and sunglasses and drive four-wheel-drive vehicles. When one leaves off, another takes up. I've seen the same van parked at the beach where I walk, every time I'm there. They probably won't approach me while I'm staying here. But I did think you should know."

He told us this a week before John and I were going on a short vacation by ourselves. The plan was to have Clara stay at home with Robert for a couple of days. She would be in school all day and with friends for the rest of the week. At 13, she was quite self-sufficient, but I felt a little apprehensive.

I asked Dr. L, the psychiatrist at the agency where I worked, if this was a dangerous situation. He assured me that it was probably fine, that most delusional people would never harm anyone around them. "Would your daughter recognize bizarre behavior?" he asked. "Would she know to call someone?" Clara would, but we decided not to warn her to do this.

We went on the trip. While we were gone she and Robert hardly saw each other.

I did what I shouldn't have. I went into his room. It smelled stale; he hadn't been sleeping on sheets lately, just on the mattress pad, like he had in San Francisco. The plastic bags and folded tissues had begun their slow accumulation. I looked in his zippered black shoulder bag: an empty three-hole notebook and 10 to 20 plastic shopping bags stuffed deliberately on each side of the bag. Tidy piles of napkins, toothpicks, and plastic tabs from bread bags were scattered among the bookshelves like small nests. A piece of paper stuck out from the dusty bookcase. The writing rambled, describing a man smoking a cigarette, a woman in a laundry…. Was Robert imagining these things, or was he out somewhere observing them? He was in a different world right among us, in the same square footage.

Later, in the mirror from the top of the hallway stairs, I saw him sitting on his bed with several long white athletic socks spread out on his legs. He smoothed them, picked them up and smoothed them again. (Where were the ones I gave him—the fancy, wool hiking socks?) "I have some thoughts about this room, if you have a moment," he said, politely, as I walked by. He told me he wanted to perhaps move the bed out, get a small sofa and an additional bookcase for books and put his clothes in this one. And he wanted to get a desk.

"I like to sit at a desk for writing. It helps to keep focus."

I made a murmuring noise, thinking of the writing I had seen earlier that morning. Did he think he was staying here forever?

John didn't understand why I couldn't be easier on him. Unlike me, John was willing to let Robert take his own slow time toward an unknown future. After all, he had gotten his driver's license; he had bought a car. Ever-so-slowly, with our prodding at each step, it was happening. So why was I so irritable, so disappointed?

John said, finally, "We have to face the fact that he's quite disabled in many ways. There's not a lot that he can actually do.

He doesn't have primary connections to anyone except us, except you. He has no idea how to maintain a relationship with anyone."

John was right. But how could Robert let it get so we were the only ones who knew him, who could help him? I was hanging on to my irritations to keep from pitying him. I wanted him fixed.

One night at the dinner table he erupted. We had been talking about the costs of things—college, student loans, medical insurance. Bored, Clara quietly cleared her plate and went upstairs.

"It's impossible, all of it!" Robert exclaimed suddenly, banging his fist on the table, nearly knocking over his glass of wine. "Completely unsustainable. How can a regular person possibly afford anything anymore?"

John made a sound of agreement and tried to say something, but Robert was on a roll. "If the smallest thing happens to you, you're out on the street. There is a responsibility—" at this he leaned in to the table, glaring, "the government has a *responsibility* to care for its citizens, and what do they do? They make everything impossible, so complicated that you can't possibly navigate it, not without a lot of money. But if you don't figure it out, if you don't comply, they harass you, they come after you… They hide the truth about what they do. They lie, and then they talk about 'responsibility' and pulling yourself up by the bootstraps. Then the public relations people come on board to make this all sound like the way-it-should-be, all fine…

"And it's bunk! It's bullshit!" Robert cupped his elbow and raised the other arm and fist up in a Fuck-You gesture, his eyes bugging, face red—someone we had never seen before. We knew he wasn't yelling at us, but there was no room for any response. We three were quiet for a few moments; then, like Clara earlier, Robert silently cleared his plate and went up to his room.

That same night I had a nightmare that I heard Robert in the hallway. In the dream, when I went to see what was happening, he was mumbling loudly to himself, his eyes wide and red like they had been at dinner. He had drawn a line on the rug in magic marker. With his foot he pushed a little notebook across the line. I picked it up and took it back into my room, surprising him—he had expected I would stay in the hallway so he could watch me read it. The notebook was filled with gibberish.

In the morning at breakfast Robert apologized. "I'm sorry about last night; it won't happen again."

Finally, at the end of the year, through a contact at church, Robert found a subsidized one-bedroom apartment in a senior housing residence in Bridgeport. It was not a great neighborhood, but the apartment was nice, and it was close to St. James. He could move in within a month, pending paperwork.

Fr. Tom also hired him part-time at St. James to do the landscaping. Now he had a place, and a job. The relief, once again, was like a blanking-out of the past nine months. "Now we'll be coming over to your place," I teased him. "You better have us over."

"I will. I will," Robert said. "It's going to be different, all of it."

Stay a Friend as Long as You Can

"... We sometimes have the wrong ideas about persons; we think that like computers they can be re-booted and something entirely new will come out: bum one day, hero the next. Well a boot won't change who I am after all these years. But I still hope. We have an obligation to hope as long as we're alive, perhaps especially when everything seems hopeless. Stay a friend as long as you can."

I have read the 40 years of journals, and what have I discovered? That I have always written about him, that he has always disappeared, right from the beginning, and I've always known it, and fought it, and been angry at him about it, in almost the same words each time. The only surprise from those excavations is how, each time Robert came back up, each time we were back in the path of our friendship, it was all new to me, a blank slate. Again and again, it was as though his disappearing into the cave of his illness hadn't happened. Others saw the pattern—*oh, that again*—but I did not. My hopefulness about Robert, about being with him, enjoying his best self with him, was like a forgetfulness, a naivete, a codependence. Perhaps it was the main way I actually loved him, in my forgetting of how he went down.

Friends have asked me why I stayed friends with him. There were so many times it would have been natural to "let go" of the relationship. I have no good answer. I clung to the friendship, and then to the idea of the friendship. Sometimes I could see that it was the clinging itself that caused much of my resentment. Yet how could I not cling? All those roles he was for me when I needed them: father, teacher, potential lover... Our relationship was burdened with an image of myself as a poet, a writer—an image we had cultivated together. Perhaps I couldn't stand for that to be a failure.

It was also hard to leave behind someone whom I knew had always felt abandoned. We had imprinted on each other in an open time in our lives. To let that go felt like too much.

Clara had a more straightforward answer. "Mom, you love him. That's why."

I was looking for the trail of that love, scared there was no evidence, no "reason" to have loved him after our first infatuation, and that perhaps I continued to relate to Robert more out of guilt than anything: He had taken care of me and I owed it to him to take care of him. And then what? Oh, I wanted much more for us than diluted charity, than do-goodness! How often I told him: "I don't want our friendship to be reduced to charity, to obligation. Isn't it more than that to both of us?" I felt that if he did not acknowledge his illness and do something about it, our friendship would become like some of those in church, available for physical assistance and prayer, but not the intimacy we had known and struggled with all these years.

I wanted *philia*, a friendship of back-and-forth, an open path, deep knowing. But that kind of love is a dance, requiring partners, and for so long my friendship with Robert had felt shadowy, hollowed-out. Who was he? He was unknowable. At any time he could become the barest trickle that would seep back into the ground. I talked while he observed. When I stopped and sat quietly with him, what I often experienced was emptiness, his emptiness. Maybe that was always so; maybe I was always talking to fill that emptiness.

Perhaps the reason I stayed Robert's friend was not, after all, something words could untangle. And who were we—where were we—without them? It was vanity and exhaustion thinking I could heal him from these voices that plagued him, from the anger and sadness that transfused him. Would the desire to love him, to be his friend, still be there if there was no hope or expectation that the man I once knew would return? Could I find the person of him—the Christ in him?

Perhaps *agape*, voluntary and unconditional love, the wide taking-in and letting-go—something you choose to do—was a miracle after all, and I had not chosen it, not yet.

God's Plan
2005

R obert's new apartment was a large one-bedroom with a wheelchair-accessible bathroom, new kitchen appliances and big windows looking out on the entrance. The brick building had once been a school and was a bit institutional, with fluorescent lights, elevators, handicap ramps, and industrial carpeting, but it was clean and quiet. As he got ready to move in, many residents had Christmas wreaths on their doors, and from the hallways there was the friendly sound of televisions and the smell of onions and garlic cooking.

Robert decided to spend some of his savings on new furniture, which he had never had. First, we bought a new double bed and box spring. A week later, we went to the IKEA store and in three hours managed to purchase everything else he wanted: bookcases, a desk, reading chair, and a red couch. For Christmas I planned to give him a portable CD player and radio, remembering that old boom box of ours that he had had for the past 10 years. He bought a cell phone; we put him on the family account and Clara showed him how to use it.

John assembled the two end tables, a small desk, and three bookcases, and together we unpacked all his books. "All the boxes have to go," John whispered to me, "even the 'good' ones," referring to the super-thick boxes Robert was so fond of, that he had hauled around since the early 70s. We could tell he was anxious about giving up the boxes, but I made jokes as we flattened and stacked them and took them out to the car. I claimed all this tossing and unpacking as my due.

"Why don't you have an open house?" I suggested. "We'll invite everyone who helped you find the apartment, everyone you know right now."

Robert liked the idea. It would be both a thank-you and a marking point. He purchased several large serving plates and bowls—bright red, green, and gold—a variety of exotic cheeses, and all the other items I had put on the list. It was much more than needed.

On a gray Sunday afternoon a couple of weeks after he moved in, about 20 people stopped by—an older woman and her daughter from the church across the street that he had met, a couple of nuns and other new friends from that church, and some of our neighbors who had gotten to know Robert over the past nine months. The apartment was crowded and lively with talk and people enjoying themselves. I felt grateful for their presence, a sign of their willingness to be involved in his life.

I stayed late after everyone left, and in the candlelight we had another glass of wine. "It went well, don't you think?" I said.

"Yes," he said, his voice soft, satisfied. "It went well. Thank you very much." He gave me one of those looks. I toasted him and looked away.

One woman at the party said she thought all that was happening with Robert was God's way, "God's plan." She said

God had a plan for all of it and we didn't know what it was; this was a chance to see it unfolding.

If I considered God as the energy that triggered Robert's calls the previous year, that prompted me into going out there, that made him receptive to our offer and to these people's offerings—then, yes, a plan unfolding. I prayed it was a good one.

After only two weeks in the new apartment, Robert went incognito. He seemed sad when he stopped by our house. When I asked he shrugged and said, "They've moved in upstairs." He told us he was going to talk to Fr. Tom and also to the building manager to tell her that there were activities upstairs that should not be going on.

Fr. Tom was straightforward. "Don't mess up a good thing," he said. "If you lose your housing, you'll be in bad shape."

In February Robert called me. "I wanted to let you know that I have heard some things recently that make me believe it is very possible I will be charged tomorrow," he said. "If that's so, I will call you. I just wanted you to be aware."

It took me a moment to understand what he meant by "charged"—I thought at first of credit cards—but then my heart sank in a familiar way when I realized he meant arrested, by Them…

"Well, you have my phone numbers," I said. It was too much work to try and discuss it with him. After these kinds of interactions, there wouldn't be a follow-up conversation. What would either of us say? *See, you were wrong?* To Robert, each thing that did not happen was just a postponement, an exacerbation—not proof that reality was different from what he suspected.

One winter evening he reluctantly agreed to go out with me to a café after the Saturday afternoon Mass. He didn't seem to know what he wanted to eat, so I ordered him a bowl of chili and a glass of wine. He was wired and disheveled.

"Things aren't good at the Parish Center," he clucked. "There's just too much to be done. I'm paid for 10 hours— Amy said they might raise that to 15—but it takes full days to get all the work done. Yesterday I was out on the north end of the church all day on the handicapped ramp, chopping ice. We had put down salt, but it doesn't touch this thick ice, and when the snow melts it drips right from the gutter so there are patches everywhere. One woman nearly fell the other day. There could easily be a hospitalization and a lawsuit. So I finally went out there with a straight hoe and just chopped. I got most of it cleared away. But there is more snow expected Monday.

"And all the plantings are a mess, just a mess," he continued, slow but obsessive. "All the trees need pruning, and I mean heavy pruning. I think the Japanese maple might not make it. The church doesn't have a decent ladder. I may have to purchase one. So that is coming up. And the leaves—even now, in the winter—piled up under everything! I'd raked them, and again, but they blow back over Main Street. It's an impossible situation, but it's got to be done. It's got to be done.

I have my list, but I'm always interrupted. Every day. 'Robert, could you help me move this; Robert could you take care of that.' I can't get my work done. I'm serious! I don't have any time or energy left afterward for anything else.

"And when I get back to my place it's usually dark, and I'm tired. There are always people in the common room, playing some game, and they try to get me to join them, but I don't. It's not for me. It's quite sad, very sad. So many of them are completely homebound, stuck there, and their families rarely ever come and visit, rarely. I do try to spend time talking with them. And that's all they really want—someone to listen to them. Someone to listen. And with winter, they never get out."

At that moment I wasn't doing a great job of listening myself. Robert had described the situation at his apartment building many times before. He had hardly touched his chili.

"I enjoyed going out with Father Malkin to give elderly people communion, when we were doing that. But he is not doing well—I don't know if I told you—he needs to take a sabbatical. And with the job, I just don't have the time. I don't have time.

"I walked to work three times this week and got a ride the other two days. It's a lousy walk; it takes about 45 minutes because of the icy patches—I have to be careful—but at the apartment I've had to dig my car out of the parking lot more than once, and when I come home at night there is no parking. So I can't lose a parking spot; it's simply not worth the aggravation. I got a ride home each night. That worked out okay."

I watched his face as he flowed along in this litany, solemn and regal, pale and fragile looking, with his coat still half-zipped and navy knit hat still sitting ridiculously atop his head like some strange knob or button. His talk came out slow and steady and irritable. He was angry about the voices we didn't believe in, about his life. I tried to interject a few times, to tell him, again, not to work more hours than he was paid for, but if he chose to do so, not to complain, but he was not listening to me that night. Perhaps the stream of talk thrust at me was a kind of punishment for not being in touch recently. I told myself to sit still, to listen to him. It was difficult; I did not succeed.

"The cardiologist says I have a heart murmur. I could die at any time," he said as we got up to leave. And yet, I thought, he refused to see a doctor for bronchitis that lingered for weeks.

"Any of us could go at any time, Robert," I replied, feeling cold and practical and stopped-up. Forget love—what was my obligation? Not to forget him, to the extent that I could. Those days it seemed that I either forgot about him entirely, or he became an object of obsession.

At least there was no talking of the voices—not that night, anyway.

His voice sounded wasted and gravelly when he called early one morning a few days later to ask if he could come over. He arrived looking pale and miserable. I called in to work to say I would be late.

"I've been up all night several nights now," he said. "They won't stop. They won't stop playing the tapes. I can't help it— I've been yelling at them. My throat is sore. My hands are sore from banging on the walls trying to get them to stop." He showed me the heels of his palms, which were red.

"Did any neighbors come out to check on you?" I asked. Didn't the noise he was making wake anyone up?

"No." He was weeping. "I just feel so bad. I have let God down. I've let him down."

"What do you mean?"

"I mean, I told God I would leave it—all this business upstairs—in his hands. That he would take care of the problem, and I would trust that he would, but I just can't—I'm anxious all the time—they're too much—persecution every night—it's so unfair; it's so unjust! I had to scream at them; I had to tell them what I think. And so I've let God down."

I asked Robert if he would consider taking something to ease his anxiety, some medication, but he didn't answer me. I knew he hated the idea of medication, that he would need such assistance. It had been a big hurdle to get him to take a non-prescription Benadryl tablet to help him sleep. Sometimes it helped; a lot of times it didn't.

"Well," I said, "You sound like you've got it figured out for God—you do your part, God, and I'll do mine and we'll fix this. Maybe God doesn't work that way. Maybe you can't sculpt it out. Maybe God doesn't make deals."

I didn't know what I was saying; I had no idea how God was working.

Robert looked at me like I had said something useful. "You mean, it's like arrogance."

Arrogance. That was exactly it. "Yes, like the voices are *yours;* they belong to you and you're going to hold on to them."

He considered that. I felt him relax a little and made him a cup of tea. As we talked, I felt an openness from him I hadn't felt in a long time. As usual, I gravitated toward that like an oasis, a mirage in the desert between us.

"I've meant to have you and John over," he said, "but I'm all messed up."

A couple of weeks later Robert brought over his important papers, a box of miscellaneous items, a stack of cash, and an extra set of keys. He was quite certain that Thursday morning he would be arrested. There was a kind of melodrama in it, as when he gave me all that cash before we left the city.

We sat in the kitchen. I cut his burrito in half since he didn't seem capable of doing that himself. He picked at his food, too anxious to eat.

"My stomach is in knots. I fully expect everything to be severely disrupted. I will possibly—likely—lose my apartment, and my job, and it will be a mess, a real mess…"

"Well, at least it will all be out in the open. Everyone will know," I said, exasperated. "What if they don't arrest you tomorrow? What about that?"

He blinked, startled by the possibility.

"Then… then I guess I'll have to start from Square One again… a different square one."

"What would that be?"

"That… well… that I made it all up." He was frowning as if this had never occurred to him.

"It wouldn't be like you 'made it up'," I said. "It's not intentional. It's real to you. Just not to the rest of the world."

This was a sting for him, I knew.

"Yet there is so much physical evidence, all their comings and goings."

Silence.

"But I'm so tired that I can't tell anymore. It's gone on too long. Why would they wait so long to do something?" We sat for a moment. "If all the things I thought were patterns weren't... But then there's all those years gone, of wasting my life…"

More silence. I stared at the table.

"You know, Robert," I said, "I didn't tell you that before I went out to bring you here I spoke to a psychiatrist about delusional disorder, which is what you have. He was impressed that you had been able to separate it out and function so well, keeping your job and such."

He was listening intently.

"They're in the way. The delusions are in our way. They're like this big roadblock in our friendship. I'm trying to respect that you're going through it, that you're experiencing this awful stuff. I feel bad and there's not a thing I can do about it. But to me it feels like you're hanging onto it."

Robert considered this for a few moments. "Perhaps I haven't been ready to give it up. I haven't been prepared enough."

Thursday, the day of the arrest, came and went. Robert left a note in our mailbox:

I saw a bright red cardinal on a bare tree top, above the parish center. Later a flock of 20-25 robins. Shepherds and flocks, the early Gospel of Spring.

I'm still having voice troubles and can't avoid worrying. Last night a very troubled sleep, even exhausted from the day's work.

Pray for me

Love R

In May we finally went together to see the psychiatrist. All the way there Robert talked minutiae: how the trees at church were trimmed, what it was like to cut boards with the head maintenance man's father, what the rectory cook said, what he ate (again) for dinner…. It was a compulsion to get all these details out; he often continued talking without any consideration of the situation, without noticing that I was trying to do something else, or not paying attention, or even falling asleep. Perhaps all the chatter was nerves about going to the doctor.

Dr. L escorted us to his third-floor office, where for an hour Robert recounted, sequentially, all the things that led up to hearing the voices, which kept him from sleeping, which kept him dreading his apartment (as it had in the city), which turned him into a vagabond, which made him depressed.

I broke in every now and then with a "Tell him about when you…" and "I was thinking you had…"

Robert said he had not heard the same cacophony of voices for a few weeks now, ever since he told them, politely, that he "wished them no ill" but they had to leave. Now there were only two voices, and he tried to persuade Dr. L and me that they were likely building maintenance people, perhaps checking up on him to see why he was making noise at night (such as yelling at the voices).

Dr. L quizzed him on the kind of voices he heard—were they muffled, like the voices outside the office right now?

"No, they're quite clear, and directly overhead, from the apartment upstairs."

Dr. L paused. "Well, since that's not really physically possible, it's likely that these new voices come from the same place as the old voices."

After many comments like, "That must be unpleasant" and "Losing sleep can really wear you down", Dr. L simply asked Robert if he wanted the voices to go away, or if he felt like he could live with them now that they weren't so threatening.

Robert considered this carefully for several minutes.

"No," he said finally. "I definitely do not want them around. I have wasted enough of my life. They are interfering with everything."

Dr. L explained that generally this kind of hearing-of-voices was unexplainable, un-analyzable, chemical. Not something one spent hours talking about one's childhood over. Robert liked hearing that; I knew he would never go into all that. He discussed medication and side effects. The doctor watched with me as Robert went through all his overstuffed coat pockets and several batches of rubber-banded cards, looking unsuccessfully for his Medicare card.

"I tell you what—you can call me with the Medicare number," Dr. L said, and wrote a prescription for a mild atypical antipsychotic.

In the car, Robert and I were both elated, like we were when we boarded the plane a year and a half ago. Was it possible that for all those depressive years he could have been taking medication that would have eased the pain instead of simply saying, "This is how I am"?

We picked up the prescription, expensive at $6 a pill—we would have to find a way to get the cost subsidized—and stopped at a Mexican restaurant where we shared a plate of enchiladas and celebrated.

For a few weeks, he was his best self—woozy for the first few days after starting the medication, he said, and his stomach growled a lot, but he slept easily for the first time in a long time. "I don't like feeling so tired, though," he told me, and I said that would probably ease up a bit when he got used to it. Even in that one week it was easier to be around him; there was less anxiety radiating from him. If it continued this way, I thought, perhaps I wouldn't dread seeing him, perhaps…

He stopped taking the medication within a couple of weeks, and the voices came back in full force, keeping him awake all night. Why did he stop? Was it too expensive? Was it not working? Perhaps Robert just went to the psychiatrist for me, as a sort of favor. In any case, his sadder self had returned.

"I know you guys don't believe it," he said, "but I'm sure, absolutely sure, that they are watching and planning. They go up and down the stairs to a boiler room that's over the apartment, and they play tapes all night long. I turn on my fans, and the radio, and I put plugs in my ears, and I am usually able to drown them out. I've covered all the unused outlets. They have fiber optics, you know. But it interrupts my sleep. It interrupts me and I get very tired. The woman who is running the investigation is very close to making an arrest."

It was the same scenario he had written about to me in San Francisco, two years earlier. As he let the story loose, Robert stretched his long arms behind his head, a gesture that looked like confidence. Part of me was glad that at least he wasn't hiding what was going on in his head, but there was nowhere to meet him in it.

A woman from church told us that Robert had been parking his car near the Parish Center and sleeping there overnight. When John went to find him to talk to him about it, he found Robert pulling onion grass on the church grounds. He complained angrily to John about the way the garden boxes were not maintained. It was the end of the workday; church staff came and went, waving goodbye at the two of them. John asked if he had been sleeping, was he depressed, and Robert suddenly erupted. "Fuck you!" he yelled. Fr. Tom had come outside by then. Robert yelled "Fuck you!" at him, too, banging his hand on the roof of his car, proclaiming that the Feds were watching him, enraged that no one believed him. John was standing too near the car door for him to get in his car and drive away, so Robert stomped off with Fr. Tom following. He came back around the other side of the rectory and started pulling grass again. As Fr. Tom approached him he strode off again down the street, "just like a crazy guy," John told me.

Fr. Tom advised John to go home. Over years of pastoral counseling he had seen situations like this many times. What would happen would happen.

Anosognosia

D on't say 'he is mentally ill'," said a friend who has been in the mental health field for his entire career. "Say 'He *has* a mental illness.' His illness is not him." I felt mildly embarrassed at this correction. Robert had a disability—like a limp, or blindness, or deafness, or a bad cowlick.

Like an albatross, like an abyss of lost-ness, like the devil. Like a friend.

But he, Robert, was not his illness. Who was he, then? Many—maybe most—of the times I saw him during those years it was hard to see anything but the illness. It wasn't like he had the illness; it was more like the illness had him. It was a wedge between us, and perhaps always had been.

Not only that, but he was never going to believe me, or anyone else, or any evidence of any sort that he had a mental illness. No matter how lovingly I explained, or whether I tried to prove it to him—*See! ALL THESE YEARS nothing "They" have said would come to pass has actually happened!* This disbelief is called anosognosia, "lack of insight"—specifically, "to not know a disease."

I only discovered this diagnosis in late 2016, in a web search on "what to do when someone who is mentally ill doesn't believe they are." I don't know whether I was relieved or more perturbed to read about this malady that goes along with the diagnosis of about half of all people who have schizophrenia or bipolar disorder, and many who have dementia or other neurological issues. The frontal lobe is damaged, physically debilitated, and the person with the illness cannot comprehend he has it.

I bought a book bluntly titled *I'm Not Sick I Don't Need Help*, by Dr. Xavier Amador, a clinical psychologist who realized he was getting nowhere in trying to convince many of his schizophrenic patients to take their medication. He asked himself why so many refused to take medication, or stopped, when it seemed obvious that medication helped them function better. Amador learned a lot by imagining himself in their position. If you don't believe you are sick, why would you take a daily medication, especially if there are side effects, like sleepiness or weight gain? When Amador realized this, he stopped trying to convince his patients of their illness and tried to find other ways to get them to accept medication, which he knew could improve or even save his patients' lives. His method is called LEAP (Listen-Empathize-Agree-Partner). As a friend or family member of someone with mental illness, you learn to take a step back and build trust by listening and asking questions without commentary. You try to find points to agree on, and then "partner" on goals you both think would be good. The mental illness does not have to be acknowledged to accomplish these goals. But because a trusting relationship has been developed, the person with mental illness might come to find the goals can be achieved more easily with medication.

It was so obvious Robert had anosognosia. What I was calling denial or stubbornness or arrogance—attributes that were definitely part of his personality—were also part of his illness. There was nothing to be said to change his mind about the "noise" and the "people" telling him things. That we could sit together and he would hear these voices and I didn't—nor did anyone else—would never be proof of anything to him. Like a developmental disability, the capacity to understand was simply not there.

But I did not know that in those first years he was with us. And he had never taken medication long enough to have a real point of comparison.

One of our neighbors who knew Robert from when he was living with us had asked him to house-sit while they were away. He came over for dinner and afterward we sat in the backyard. John and I had thought perhaps house-sitting would be a reprieve for him, but Robert told me that They had been harassing him at the neighbor's house: every time he came in, the phone would ring and continue to ring every five minutes while he was in the house.

"It's a fact."

At his apartment, They had moved out temporarily, mandated by an "injunction" of some sort. Robert believed that Fr. Tom had arranged this. He said that They had discovered some kind of agent in the apartment upstairs, someone highly unusual, that They "couldn't touch." A big mistake had been made, but to "close the case" they had to "make restitution." They had told Robert to go to City Hall for this restitution, but he refused. He knew that once they had him in a room they could "do anything they want."

"So they've followed me here." The usual silence fell between us like a stone. Dusk was coming on and the features of his face across from me in the backyard were dimming. I heard him sigh loudly. "You think these people don't exist?" he said angrily. "That they don't do these things?"

I sighed back at him. "I believe there are people who do these things, but not to you." A tension was building inside me. "Did you get my letter? The one I sent last month?" On Palm Sunday I had sent him a long letter, pleading with him to acknowledge his illness and how it had come between us. It was a letter that said "everything," as plainly and lovingly as I could. Long ago, it would have brought us together.

"I received your letter," he said, coldly, "but I didn't read it. I knew what it said and I didn't want to get into it."

He would have it his way no matter who reached out to him.

"I am so tired of this," I yelled, suddenly. "I am so fucking tired of it. You are textbook delusional! There are hundreds of thousands of people suffering the same things you are. Why are you so fucking special? You just isolate yourself!"

In all the years I had known him, I had never really yelled at him, and it was an overflowing. It felt good; it felt horrible.

His face was closed and cold.

"You have the opportunity to not be isolated!" I said. "You choose to stay stuck. You choose it, over and over again."

I stood up abruptly from the lawn chair. "Goodbye, Robert," I said. "Goodbye." The words coming out of my mouth were like a door slamming. I left the yard and went into the house. Then he got up—I could see him from the kitchen window—and went back to the neighbor's house. About 20 minutes later I walked over there in the dark. His car was in the driveway, but no lights were on. He was in there in the dark, in his delusions, wavering in and out of self-pity, suffering.

I counted the times he was about-to-be-arrested since he had moved out of our house: February, July, August, September, October, December, April, July, December. On the Wednesday after New Year's 2007 he called, cheerful, to tell me They had agreed to a meeting, with witnesses and a lawyer if we liked, next Tuesday. He gave me a specific room in the Federal building downtown. Were John and I available to go?

"Of course." These were the cycles of the story. There would be no meeting, and no convincing him.

Undone
2007

John woke me up at midnight. "You'd better get up." I practically jumped out of bed and got dressed quickly. I knew it was him, about him. I should have known the phone call from him that morning was a trigger, a foreshadow.

Clara was on her way to bed. "I heard Robert down there," she said. "He's really upset." She paused, shrugged. "Good luck with that."

Robert had arrived an hour before at the door to John's office in the garage, crying, trembling, wearing only his pants— no shirt or socks or shoes—in the cold January night. His chest was covered with blood. John told me later that it was shocking and frightening; for a moment he thought Robert had been shot. He sat him down to investigate the injuries: a gash to the chin (the source of all the blood), scrapes across his entire chest, skin ripped on both palms and a gouge on his left foot. John walked him carefully down the driveway in a pair of my shoes, cleaned him up in the kitchen, and gave him a shirt to wear.

I put my hand on Robert's shoulder. He was crying, pleading. One of the voices had told him he must leave his apartment immediately. Run. A "madman" chased him all the way to his car and had followed him here.

"Call the police," he said, urgently. "Call them. They know what's happening. Tell them my name. They'll know. They've been investigating the investigators. They know everything. They'll know about the madman who was after me."

Dr. L had told me a while ago that if the police get involved they can get a person hospitalized. I could see this might be our opportunity, but how could we call the police, knowing they'd take Robert away not to help catch his killer, but to detain and contain his delusions? It felt like too big a betrayal. (John admitted later that he was just too tired to deal with a whole night in the waiting room at the hospital.)

Robert was listening, head cocked. He was hearing the voices as we sat here at the table with him. Calmly, he asked me to please go to the upstairs bathroom and check for the madman.

"He's going to kill my friend Corinne. He's going to shoot her."

Although he didn't leave his chair Robert was agitated, blinking and weeping, hearing something unfold in his mind.

"He's killed her. Oh, he's killed her! And he's going to kill me. He says he's going to get me in the church parking lot tomorrow afternoon and shoot me 23 times."

He was crying, clutching himself tightly. I was glad that his hallucinations were auditory and not visual. He calmed a little.

"The police are going to come. They're going to come for him. We'll wait for them."

After a long minute of silence, John said, "You realize we do not hear anything, don't you?"

He nodded but was completely distracted by what he was hearing. John made tea; I got Robert some ibuprofen and a clean sock for his uninjured foot. We sat in silence for 15 minutes or so, then he asked me to look out the front door. The street was dark and silent.

After another half hour we decided that Robert should try to sleep on the couch. I would sit up with him while John went to bed. I busied myself gathering sheets and pillows and a quilt and setting up the couch. He lay down carefully. I put a pillow under his injured foot. I turned on the Christmas tree lights and settled in the chair across the room pretending to rest, closing my eyes to a slit as I watched him fall asleep. The cat jumped onto the couch with Robert and sat near his head on top of the cushion, like a guardian.

It was a vigil.

"Don't fall asleep with your glasses on," he warned me, out of nowhere.

After a quarter-hour he began to snore lightly. I worried he might leave if I went up to bed and then remembered that he had no shoes. In some way Robert had guaranteed himself a night on the couch, or a night in the hospital; in some way this was what he wanted. Lying on the couch so pale and still, he looked like a corpse. I thought of what it would be like when he died; what it would be like tomorrow: what-next-what-next-what-next. Would we be able to get him into a hospital? Would he self-check into one? He cannot stay here.

My thoughts were very pragmatic, very utilitarian.

Finally I got up to bed for a ragged sleep. When Clara awoke I explained the situation to her and told her she could eat breakfast in her room if she preferred. She was used to Robert. She seemed to expect his breakdowns and did not understand them, but she did not worry about it; she saw him as our friend.

I didn't want to be alone with Robert, so John skipped work, calling in a "family emergency," and we both sat in the living room with him for an hour or so. Robert said that everything would be okay; John said in his teacher mode, "I don't think so. And by coming here like you have, you've lost some of your autonomy." After a while we let him go back to sleep.

I put in a call to Robert's supervisor at the church, and to the psychiatrist, who told me the hospital wouldn't take him anyway, not if he wasn't an overt threat to himself or others. "Even if he was admitted," Dr. L said, "it would be a short fix. They'd sedate him, and he wouldn't like that, and then he'd be discharged within 24 hours, probably. He has to want treatment for anything to work."

John and I went out to the garage, where Robert could not hear us, to confer about what to do next. I did not want him sleeping here again tonight, I said; it didn't feel right. It was as though this time, unable to keep the voices in his container anymore, he had brought them with him and there were now too many people in the house.

"You can tell him if he wants I'll stay with him at his place tonight," I said.

I drove to his apartment to retrieve his keys, cell phone, and some clothes. I was anxious as I unlocked the door, but the accumulation of papers and books was only two years' worth. There were the familiar bags, both paper and plastic, everywhere. And there were the bags within the bags, some containing other items (bandaids, socks, old newspapers, new books) and some just containing more bags.

I wandered the three rooms of his apartment, taking it in. The books in the bookcases looked hopeful, like we were that day when we had the move-in party. The bathroom was clean. There was that ratty, blue, inside-out T-shirt on a hanger—how he loved that shirt! The kitchen was filthy, but not from food, just dust accumulation. One clean glass rested upside down on a folded paper towel.

I realized that I came here also to see whether I could spend the night without feeling frightened, but his place was innocuous, without threat.

When I got back home, Robert was up and eating some soup. We sat around some more, in silence. There was no other subject, none of the familiar bantering between us as though what had happened was not profound. "You need to call the psychiatrist," I said. "He's expecting a call from you." We watched as he did this.

When John took him to the clinic to check out his wounds, I swabbed down the bathroom where the cut on Robert's chin had split open again, and put the bloodied quilt and sheets in the wash with stain remover. I swept and vacuumed and took a shower and tried without success to rest.

They were back after two hours; the injuries were minor. Robert had asked John whether he could stay at our house again that night, but John told him I would stay with him at his place instead and he agreed. We didn't talk about why we were doing anything.

After dinner I drove us both to his apartment. Robert went straight to bed. I stayed up for another hour or so and gave a quick mop to his kitchen floor, which was too dirty to walk on in socks and certainly not in bare feet. The windows were open a crack because the building heat, not adjustable, was too high. The noise of the nearby thruway was continual: trucks downshifting, the revving of an occasional speeding car.

I set up the camping pad and blanket I had brought on the floor and listened to his light snores from the other room for quite a while before I drifted off. I left a light on. I didn't want to be in the dark with him.

At 1:15 I heard the bed squeak and as he came out of his room I gave him a friendly wave, hoping he wouldn't be startled to find me there. "I will have a surprise for you in the morning," he said in that decisive delusional voice that I had come to hate.

"Have you been sleeping?" I asked.

"No," he said, "I've been listening to the tapes." Then he went into the bathroom.

When he came out again he paused and said, "In the morning. A tape. It's good."

He didn't sleep again until later. I heard him stir, but no deep breathing. I was grateful he wasn't talking out loud. I was scared, I realized. All my pragmatism would not dissolve this hole of the night and his strangeness. I couldn't trust what he would do next, and I wouldn't be able to understand any of it.

I would just have to be scared.

There was a small relief in knowing that my presence did not stop the voices, that I couldn't fix anything and was therefore not responsible.

I slept and woke, slept and woke. At about 8 I heard him get up and dress. He put on his coat and whispered to me that he would be back in a few minutes. I remembered he didn't have his car, so he would indeed be back, and it occurred to me that he was going to check outside or downstairs for the cassette tape he talked about in the middle of the night.

I lay there until he came back empty-handed, then I rose and put on my clothes and stood in his doorway. He was sitting on the end of his bed.

"Do you want to go out and get something to eat?" I suggested.

"Yes."

When I finished folding my blanket and pad, Robert was still sitting on the bed. He looked up at me, then down, his hands between his knees, dejected.

"They're telling me now that it's all in my head. I guess they've been trying to tell me that for a long time, giving me clues, but now it's in plain English. We're in your head; take the pills and we'll go. We'll miss you, but we'll go."

He had given names to the two remaining voices: Frank Fisher and Corinne Cortalano. Corinne was the one who was shot the night before last when he showed up at our house, he said.

"They are my friends. They are friendly voices. But they are both dead. That should have been a clue, but I just accepted it and so made them alive, in a way. Frank committed suicide."

I sat down on the side of his bed near him. The room was very dim and gray, like the January morning outside. He laid back on the pillow and began to weep silently as he talked, his voice so soft I could hardly hear him.

"There are so many people who see and hear things like I do, so many young people, who kill themselves. It's so very sad. At one point I was keeping track of how many suicides there were from the Golden Gate Bridge—hundreds—remember?"

I nodded.

"It's so real, so real; it's hard to accept that it's in my head. But they're telling me it is. And they're also telling me... that I did this to myself. That if I take the pills they'll leave and go to someone else who's self-destructive."

"To help or harm that other self-destructive person?"

"Both, I guess."

I sat quietly beside him.

"I'm in my head; I'm always in my head; they're in my head... but if they go maybe they will come into my heart. They're good friends; I trusted them... but Frank lied to me. He told me to run. Corrine told me that egomaniac, that crazy man—he was a professional killer—was on his way to kill me. Frank just said Run. And I grabbed my pants and ran out the side door... I didn't even put on my pants until I was outside and then I ran to my car over on Union Street, and then I fell. It was like someone tripped me. I fell and then I drove to your place...."

He sighed deeply, still weeping. "But now I've hurt myself. I've hurt myself. Now they're talking to me in plain English: take the pills. We'll miss you. That's what the tape was saying, 'I'll miss you, I'll miss you,' over and over again. I thought, if I can get the tape then it'll be proof—you'll know this is so—but..."

"No tape."

"There was no tape. No cassette. I didn't get the clues." He paused. "It's very hard. Very hard to understand."

"Listen," I said, trying for a light tone, "There are hundreds of thousands of people who hear and see things—maybe not as interesting or complex as you—but who are tormented and persecuted the same way you have been. It's mental illness. It's not you; it's your illness."

Robert was quiet for a bit. Tears were rolling out the corners of his eyes. Then he said, "Maybe this is really good that this happened."

"Maybe."

"Maybe I can get them out of my head and into my heart."

"Maybe. 'Them' is you, you know. You."

"I've always been in my head. Always."

"Yes. You need help getting out. And you need help learning how to take help."

As I sat on the bed with him, he gradually became happier. His face shifted, first focused and then bewildered, like he was understanding something, like something was dawning on him.

But now I was an observer more than a participant. The past three years had worn me down; I was wary and tired. For how long would he understand that the voices were in his head? He'd get the pills, perhaps. But how long would he take the medication? How long before the next cycle pulled him down and away? This was it, likely. The years left to us marked with this coming together and this coming undone.

I thought of when I pulled up in the rental car to get him in San Francisco and we had driven together like two new people to the airport. I told myself to enjoy these moments with him, just now, just as they were, but it was hard.

We got up. I helped him soak and bandage his foot, slowly and carefully, at his pace.

"Frank is telling me to take the meds…. Corinne knows where everything is; she helps me find things. Oh God—will I now have to listen to the others and hear their opinions and thoughts on everything?" But I could tell Robert was relieved to let Them out a bit.

We bought more bandages at the pharmacy and then I drove us to the diner, where we had a two-hour breakfast, a current of good talk between us like the old days, and he paid.

Ten Years
2007-2017

Anyone who understood mental illness would know, of course, that Robert's breakdown, his coming undone, or even our intimate conversation that morning in his apartment was not the "end" of anything, or even the beginning of anything. The ten years following were marked by the milestones of Easter, Thanksgiving and, usually, his birthday. Clara's graduation from high school, and college. His presence in our lives was a constant background hum—was he up, was he down, what should we do next? Usually the "doing" amounted to inviting him to dinner, and an occasional day trip somewhere. Robert's delusions were a disability that I learned to live with, as he had, giving in to the lack of predictability of his moods, then also of his capabilities. For someone so efficient, so preemptive and ahead of things, I was always behind his illness. Like him, I didn't believe it sometimes. Mental illness makes you doubt everything, all the time. I hate that.

No One is Named Marvin Anymore

After Robert came undone that January, he went back to Dr. L and renewed his prescription, or so he said. We were in touch with him most every week, either at Mass or having him over for dinner. It was hard to spend just an hour or so with him; he required several hours before he would relax.

Once afterward he called to say he had left his little plastic packet with his driver's license and debit card in it at our house and would come by to pick it up. He said he had also left a plastic bag with books in it. I opened the bag, and of course it was stuffed with many more plastic bags, some empty envelopes, folded paper towels, and a measuring cup. I put the three books and cup into one bag and tossed the extra bags as John watched.

"I can't believe you're doing that," he said.

"Yeah, well," I said.

About a minute later Robert called. His voice was very cheerful and strange. He said that a "new friend" was going to pick up the books. "He's coming to that area anyway so he said he'd pick them up. He'll come to the door, identify himself, and get the stuff. His name is Marvin."

I should have known that no one was named Marvin anymore, and no "friends" come out at 9 p.m. to drive five miles to pick up a bag of books. But while Robert was on the phone I believed him. I believed him because I didn't want to suspect everything he said was prompted by the voices. Once the suspecting started, everything would be suspect.

Oh, Marvin, come here! Come in and talk to me, would you? Maybe Marvin could add some substance to my poor friend Robert.

Quite a Day

One Wednesday in July I received two phone messages from St. James staff. Robert had almost been arrested at Sikorsky

Airport, a small municipal airport a couple of miles from church, where he had somehow gotten through security and was wandering around the airplanes, a duffle bag in tow. The head of airport security was called, as well as both the Bridgeport and Stratford police. Robert tried to call John but couldn't reach him. He then told the police to call St. James, and two staff members, Sr. Julie and Therese, came down to retrieve him.

This was possibly the very scene Robert had imagined for the past several years, like a drug bust, surrounded by four cop cars who opened all his car doors and searched for clues. Robert told them that someone had come by the parish—not a parishioner—begging for a ride to the airport, and that he had been ripped off—his money, credit card, and keys stolen. But there on the airport tarmac, his wallet was in his pocket, and when at Julie's request he checked, he had his money and cards. He swore his keys had been stolen but refused to look for them. The cops did not ticket or book him, but they made everyone wait for paramedics who checked Robert's vital signs then let him go with Julie and Therese, who drove his car home for him. He refused to go back to the Parish Center, where he could have rested and would not be alone.

Robert called us after an hour or two. He said he had tried to call Dr. L, but who knows whether he would get a call back—it was so hard to get through the system to reach the doctor.

"It's been quite a day," I said, glad that he had called the psychiatrist of his own accord.

"Yes, but we don't have to go into that now. Everything's okay," he said. "Everything's good."

I was quiet. "It doesn't sound so good to me."

"Well, it's okay. Everything's good." He had on his best calm friendly voice, the Marvin voice. As he was losing himself, I was losing him, too.

One Fine Day

For the first time in a long time, I got him to come along with me for the day to the Clark Art Institute in northwestern Massachusetts. I have gone there with my favorite people; Robert and I had visited once before. The long, three-hour drive up Route 8 through Connecticut and into the Berkshires is part of the leisure of the day. I picked him up at his apartment with coffee for us both. He was in one of his solemn moods; I could feel it as he got into the car. His first complaints were about the disadvantages of his neighborhood.

"There is no place to go for a walk, or even to pick up a paper or a cup of coffee," he said. "You have to drive everywhere. Many of the seniors are home-bound. They don't do anything all day except watch television."

When he talked like this, there was a sense that in some way his dissatisfaction was our fault, for not letting him live in our house. I had said this to him once and he had paused, considered, and said, "No, that's not how I meant it."

I listened and drove.

We stopped in Pittsfield at a funky diner that boasted the best sausages in Massachusetts. Over breakfast we talked again about what was happening to him. In his apartment, he said, he ate his mash of canned salmon, tuna and beans ("for protein") quickly, in the dark. He couldn't stand to be there anymore since they were always monitoring him, so he was sleeping on a couch in the common room of the building where the residents played cards. A janitor knew he did this but left him alone.

Robert shrugged. "I guess I never really gave up on them being there."

My disappointment rose, a familiar agita. "So when you said last year if they didn't arrest you, you'd have to begin again, 'at square one,' were you just saying that to please me?"

"No." He poked at his pancakes.

His face was haggard; he was suffering. His story was filled with jagged edges, one day believing something different from the next; one day hopeful, the next day not. The delusions weren't something you could proclaim, *Alleluia, it's over!*

"It just makes me... so sad," I said, exasperated. "It seems like it's yourself you can't live with, in your home, with your things around you... And I can see that the idea of it all being *in you* might be more frightening than having federal agents harassing you." He was listening. I ploughed ahead. "It's like you're not ready to give it up." I hesitated. "Not that you can 'give up' the voices—they're real to you—but you're miserable and you know it and you won't do anything about it. You claim to trust John and me, your friends, but you don't. Not really. And the fact that you think you can get rid of the voices without medication—that's part of the delusions, too. It buries us both."

There. I was relieved of the burden of my speech of the day. Robert was quiet, rather than defensive. That was the advantage of a couple of hours behind us and a day's worth of hours ahead. Time to leave conversations unresolved.

The day had started cloudy, but there was a crack of turquoise overhead and gradually the sky cleared. By the time we were out of Pittsfield on Highway 7 in that wonderful valley alongside Mt. Greylock, it was crystal clear.

The Clark Art Museum is set in a field just outside Williamstown. It is small, as museums go; you sense that there will be time to visit every painting you want, and so the panic I sometimes feel going into a museum is calmed and time opens up. *I can spend the whole day here*, I always think with pleasure. Mid-week, the museum is also quiet; more than once I have been the only viewer in the room with the Renoir, and the bronze Rodin ballet dancer, standing at attention. A huge open field—a cow pasture, actually—with woods and a walking trail is part of the grounds.

After an hour and a half of wandering in the museum, first together, then separately, Robert and I took a break and hiked up the hill into the pasture, where I put out my jacket and lay in the damp grass for half an hour or so and gazed up at the sky, now a depth-less blue. The spring sun was perfectly warm. I closed my eyes and rested. I heard Robert walk off a bit, then come back.

The day assumed its rhythm. We were light with each other, making little jokes—this, the particular pleasure of spending an extended period of time with him. Circling back, we came upon five trees that had grown together, maple and birch, so that the bark was either white with ragged vertical gray striations of the maple, or gray, with the circular smooth texture of birch. In one tree, a huge birch branch was attached midway with the maple, like two huge maple-birch lips.

The field below was soggy from snow and a week of rain, and the gully was filled with frogs. We couldn't see them, but the noise of the peepers was like a chorus of smoke alarms, piercing enough to hear all the way up the hill. As we stomped through, they stopped their peeping, going silent as suddenly as they had started. We stayed by the gully until they tentatively began again.

The day was this way—booming, blue, promising... a feeling that it could go on and on: one of those fine days. I did not worry what Robert was thinking, or what I thought about him, a reprieve from the past erosive year.

On the way home we stopped for dinner at a Thai restaurant, teasing each other; we laughed about his "problem."

"What a huge capacity you have for constructing all these worlds and patterns in your head," I said. At that point I still thought he was in denial about his delusions, and that denial was for me the biggest problem. It seemed to me if he could accept the fact that he was having delusions, and do something about it, we could all learn to live in it and still have good days like this one. When he refused, I couldn't coddle the unreality of his inner world, and we were at an impasse.

Robert smiled at me. "Why can't a counselor talk with me the way you do?"

"Because you won't let them." We let that fact sit between us. "Perhaps I should go to therapy with you, and be your interpreter," I said. "I could say, 'I speak his language.'" I paused. "Then they'd probably medicate me." We both laughed.

A Pile of Peanuts and a Prayer Garden

I was between jobs and had more time, so I tried to vary my visits with him. One day I bought some sandwiches and took them to St. James to eat lunch with him. Robert was kneeling on the sidewalk near the grass outside the church. I stopped near him where he had set a pile of peanuts in the grass and was carefully breaking one into crumbs on the sidewalk.

"A squirrel comes out here for the peanuts," he explained to me, pleasantly, without looking up, as though we were casual acquaintances, "and now a jay is out, and these are for some sparrows."

"A regular St. Francis situation," I said. "I brought you a sandwich. Would you like to have some lunch with me?"

It was peaceful at the picnic table behind the Parish Center. Robert continued to act very distant from me while I acted more and more friendly.

"I have an idea for the space back here," he said, finally. He got up and paced the rectangle of the lawn, which was bordered by some withering conifers. "I think this space can be a Prayer Garden, where people can come and meditate. A few shade trees will be required," he said. And requisitioned and paid for, I thought, cynically. "And perhaps a stone bench, and a statue of the Blessed Virgin."

Who was the "Blessed Virgin" to him? I didn't know. But I continued to brainstorm with him.

"How about just putting out a couple of chairs under the tree, like a praying zone, an altar of nature, and see what happens?" I said, inspired. "That's what I would do. Put some attention into that one spot, and people will come."

I was hoping my little burst of energy about the project would break through, but Robert just smiled weakly, finished his sandwich, and said he had to go back to work. This was different, him making the first move to leave. It did not bode well, I thought. If he closed us off we wouldn't have the option of asking him questions—was he hearing the voices, was he taking his meds, did he fill out the forms I'd given him to get discounts on medication, etc.

"Well, I'll come by again soon," I said.

A couple of weeks later I found him at church in the late afternoon at church, raking. He was surprised to see me.

"Let's go out to dinner!" I suggested.

He looked at me, then away, as if considering his calendar. "That would be fine. I have to finish raking, though." I knew he didn't have to finish, but I didn't resist him. *Go ahead, be obsessive*, I thought, as I stood in the shade and watched him. *I've got all the time in the world today.*

We went to a restaurant in Milford and stayed until 9:30, enjoying one of our good talks, in which he talked almost as much as me and we didn't probe the Sad Sack stuff—no disabilities, no mental illness, no chores-that-have-to-be-done.

"I'm writing about us," I confessed. "It's the story of our friendship. But I don't think I'd ever want you to read it. And that's pretty weird."

He studied me for a moment, impassive. "I'm glad you're working. You'll need a good reader," he said, solemnly. I was relieved that he seemed to like the idea that I was writing about us. "You don't need to tell me anything about it," he said. "Just ask me if you need anything."

I said I would, although I was not sure what he meant.

A couple of weeks later he was down again. I had called him twice inviting him to dinner, got his voicemail, gave up. When I saw Robert midweek alongside the apple bin at the grocery store, looking beat in his dirty, long-sleeve T-shirt, fleece vest, and ruffled hair, I could not resist says, "So, instead of going out to dinner, we meet at Trader Joe's." He was just getting off work trimming trees or mowing the St. James lawn, I guessed. His face was so thin, his skin discolored from too much sun, like he was 84 instead of 74. He shrugged. Who knew whether he missed the calls, or chose to ignore them? There was no trusting any of that anymore.

Easter After Easter

Since I had joined the church in 1999, Holy Week each year for us had become like a short three-day journey outside time. I would usually sing with the choir, and Robert and John, both great lectors, were often called upon to read for one of three services. Fr. Tom's Easter homily was repeated in slight variations on Holy Thursday, Good Friday, and Easter. The pattern of Holy Week, he said, is the pattern of Christ: loving others even though you know they will hurt you; offering no resistance, no violence, even when you have the power; offering yourself up to death—all the daily deaths of self—and rising after, rising through death, because "love never ends."

Did love never end, really? It sounded so true and natural in the beautiful Easter-lit church, but outside of that place I felt ends and stops everywhere. As John and I arrived at Holy Thursday Mass, we saw Robert on the side aisle scoping out the pews in the back of the church.

A couple of weeks earlier as I drove home from work one evening along Mill River I had seen a man walking along the sidewalk by the river. He looked homeless, wearing a knit cap, big boots, dirty pants, and skiing gloves, his gait swingy and loose. It was a moment before I realized it was Robert. He had told us he would often drive from his apartment to walk in Fairfield.

Now in church he appeared to be wearing the same outfit, his brown winter hat resting like a chocolate drop on his head, giant gloves stuffed into his coat pockets. We waved. Scowling, he put his hand up briefly as if to keep us out of his vision. Then he headed up, all business, to the sacristy, probably to see whether a Eucharistic minister was needed, or just to get away from the possibility of having to see or deal with us.

But I, too, did not want to deal with him. When I'd seen Robert walking by the river I thought, *Did he see me?*, then, *Is he planning to come by our house? I hope not!*; then, *Why can't you just let him be?* (perhaps I was like one of the voices that wouldn't leave him alone…); then, *Would it be so hard for you to include him in your life? What kind of a so-called Christian are you?* It was a real question, not rhetorical.

"I'm not sitting with him," I said suddenly to John. "I'm not going anywhere near him." John shrugged, but he, too, could see what kind of a place Robert was in. Little surges of irritation ebbed and flowed through me all during Mass. At that service at St. James, in imitation of Jesus at the Last Supper, everyone was encouraged to have their feet washed, not just 12 members of the congregation. Chairs and bowls of water and clean towels were set up in the center aisle and priests, staff, and other volunteers served anyone who sat in front of them. It was surprising how this gesture of vulnerability opened people up. Most people would much rather be foot-washers than have their feet washed—easier to serve than to receive. In this mood, I knew I would not be able have my feet washed, to offer myself, to be served. Nor, I assumed (I refused to look), could Robert.

In the line for communion he ignored us, looking elderly and frail, hungry. When he ignored me like this, it felt worse than his disappearing. He was like a hand right up in front of my face. I couldn't see anything, not the hand nor what was behind it.

What movement made me relent? I sent him a card the next day, inviting him to Easter dinner. To my surprise, Robert called on Saturday and said he would come. I set the table, and when he didn't arrive at the appointed time (did I really expect him to come?) I quietly removed his table setting into the kitchen, where it was like a solitary memorial: the porcelain plate with its delicate flower print, the silver utensils, the white cloth napkin, the gold-rimmed goblet.

Midway through dinner he showed up, somewhat disheveled. John said he had probably been in his car somewhere, parking out the holy day, perhaps by the beach where he liked to watch the terns and gulls doing their dances.

"How are you, how are things," he mumbled tonelessly after dinner, as he went through the small stack of his mail that still came to our house.

"They're fine," I said. "How are things with you?"

"It appears I don't know much about anything." His voice was very flat. It occurred to me later that the voices had probably told him the Bad People would be arrested, and then they weren't.

"Well, it's good you're here." That statement was my Easter moment, I supposed, along with inviting him in the first place. All morning Fr. Tom had preached *You can choose to do the more loving thing*. At any time, not on your own but with the power of God, you can choose to change the notes. He meant the single-piano-note motif that tends to go bang-bang-bang during family gatherings where someone was behaving… like Robert.

And so it was good he came; he had a hot meal, and a glass and a half of good wine, and laughed a few times. Fr. Tom has also said *You have to live in the present—if you live in the future, you're always worried and anxious; if you live in the past you're always pissed off, grudgeful. Whichever, past or future, you miss what's in front of you.*

I was grieving Robert as though he were gone. Grieving him was grieving me, that young me we created together. Who knew the stages of denial and anger, unfolding and refolding, would take so long? I wanted another, different stage of grief to come upon me, while we were both still alive.

After dinner, he lingered and talked while I cleaned the kitchen. The wine had helped to loosen him up. When it was quite late, and I needed to get to bed, I walked him to his car. The stars had come out.

The week after, he came by and left Mary Oliver's latest book, *Red Wing*, on the kitchen table with a note. A peace offering.

A Last Speech

He called and left a message, his voice cracking, "Things have been going on—it's, just, well, unexplainable. I won't go into that business. I just wanted to thank you, to thank you so much for all you've done for me over the past few years, and always. I love you. I just wanted to thank you, to say that."

It was a like a Last Speech. I was nervous calling him back. "Thank you for the thank-you. And you're welcome. Sometimes you're more welcome than others," I said, trying to joke, "but you are welcome." Pause. I was getting better at pauses. "So are you taking the meds?"

"I'm sleeping," he said, not responding to my question. "Yes. Except for a few instances. But I'm sleeping."

To me this meant he probably wasn't taking the meds. He was experimenting to see what he could get away with, I thought, skipping a day here or there, since the voices were not going away. Or maybe he didn't even really want them to.

And probably the medication wasn't right. If he had even the slightest enthusiasm about it, I thought, I would be pushing him to call Dr. L to work on it, again. But Robert would wait so long because he didn't want to call him (okay, who would?), and then he would stop taking them altogether (although that time he said they really did help him sleep, which might be an incentive) and we would go through this cycle. If it played out as before, he would disappear for a few weeks. He would go to work, but he wouldn't call anyone; people from church would ask John and me about him, why he was so distant. Or he would do something dramatic.

He thanked me again and I was silent. Then he said, "Don't worry, I'm not going to do anything"—meaning, I took, not hurt himself.

Hopes and Shoulds

For Christmas we gave him a new cell phone with big buttons. Kevin, who now lived in San Francisco and was home for the holiday week, programmed the phone and showed Robert how to use it. He was so happy to see Kevin; I could see it from comments he made about whether Kevin would rise in the company where he worked as an audio engineer, traveling all around, whether he might invent something.... Ah, I thought to myself, washing another pot, listening to Robert in the other room, he has shifted his dreams and hopes and interests to my son. My daughter-like sulkiness, rising again.

Robert talked, again, of working less now that it was winter, of getting up early, exercising, doing some reading. "There are some things I'd like to write," he said. With much ado, he had purchased a lot of books and now intended to read them and perhaps "give a class" at St. James. How hopeful he could be, over and again. Why would I hold his aspirations and illusions against him? I knew I should be pleased he was in a hopeful place at the moment. It was just light conversation, which is what we had with each other.

After the Saturday afternoon Mass, I made a routine of staying behind to see him, just for a short chat. I would always be very conscious as to where he was sitting. More than once he was kneeling just a couple of pews ahead of me, eyes closed, lips moving. I waited for him after everyone left while he went pew to pew in his post-Mass ritual, straightening the hymnals and picking up discarded bulletins and scraps of paper. He had been ignoring me again the past several months, so he didn't look in my direction, and if our eyes caught, he would not return my smile. I would pretend we didn't see each other. This was our new little game, our awkward pretense. There was a silliness in it, and an anxiety.

On Tuesday evenings he was attending Education Parish Service classes, staying behind to talk to the professor about the Old Testament or Vatican II. He needed the recognition and attention. *You see, I am a former scholar. I know how to think about these things. I know what they really mean.* Even though his pronouncements were convoluted and twisty and did not make sense, it was still a worthy activity and got him out of his apartment. St. James paid the fee for the courses, a recompense for all the extra hours he worked at church.

There was now a whole cadre of people at St. James who knew Robert as a kind, elegant, eclectic, hard-working, spiritual man. Sometimes I would see him greet others, mostly elderly people whom he knew from daily Mass. He had become someone who said, "God bless you" rather than goodbye. They always smiled when he clasped their hands. I watched him and realized I was jealous of the attention he gave them.

"He's a holy man," I heard one person say. That was Robert's mystique, never-ending. Sometimes I wanted to claim him back, to say "I knew him when!", or "You don't know him!" One time a woman was telling Robert "what a gift" he was to the parish, with all his hard work and his kindness and attention to the grounds. She saw me standing nearby and introduced us. "Virginia, do you know Robert?" she asked, extending her arm to bring us together. He and I both smiled, and she apologized, remembering from somewhere that we were acquainted, "Oh, of course you know each other! How could I forget!"

Mostly I was more and more grateful that these others besides me were in his life. Their love, light as it was, sustained him, made him feel useful and respected. For months at a time it kept him steady—sometimes, even, approachable and friendly. If he kept this up long enough, I thought, we could forget those delusional episodes ever happened. He never referred to them.

One time when the church was finally empty, I made my way toward him, smiling like any other friend. We hugged, then he excused himself to lock the church doors. "Father will be asking me, any minute now," he anticipated. On cue, the priest inquired whether Robert had locked the door yet or not—his unofficial, probably self-appointed, duty. I sat down again while he finished. He was thinner than I'd ever seen him, and his clothes were dirty after having worked in them all week, but today his face was relaxed, and when he finally sat down in the pew behind me he looked me in the eye and it was a kind look.

"How are you doing?" I asked.

"It's been very busy," he said, sighing. He was still working at least 30 hours a week at the church. I knew staff had given up trying to get him to leave earlier, and so they just thanked him when they could. I often reminded him that the amount of time he put in at St. James was his choice, that no one expected it of him, and that he shouldn't complain about his own choice. But not that day. That day I was just going to try and keep all my hopes and shoulds at bay. I wasn't going to worry about how well he had been taking care of himself, or not, or how hard he had been working, or whether I should invite him to dinner. I was just going to sit there and listen.

"I took care of the front area this week," he began, and told me, again, in elaborate detail about the pruning and shaping of the trees in front of the rectory and parish center, the failing or flourishing of the annuals on the side of the church, the antics of that damn squirrel that he'd been feeding for the past year. As he talked, his thin arms lifted and gestured, lanky and eloquent. This was his offering, this rumination. This was him, now, talking about himself.

After he talked about the grounds for a while, he paused, then said that for his birthday the office secretary had made Robert a big "cake" out of fruit: apples and oranges and bananas. We laughed.

I shifted my position but did not make a move to leave. *Stay*, I said to myself. *Stay out of yourself, stay with him.* Then he talked more personally, about how he was feeling physically, how much sleep he'd been able to take in. He went to bed quite early, he said, around 9:30, sometimes taking "a pill"— probably the Benadryl—and he would sleep for a while, but awaken at least twice each night and it was hard to get back to sleep. His best sleep was from 4 to 8 in the morning, which meant he came in later to work and he didn't like that.

"But your job is flexible," I reminded him as I had many times, "You can come in later, so do it. Do what makes you feel best." I also told him I had read that sleep patterns change dramatically as we got older.

Another pause. Then he asked me about Kevin in California, and Clara, who would soon be going to college. I updated him like I would any friend, told him I was worried about her driving, about the cost of college, about what would happen. He nodded, listening. I felt the familiar pull to talk more to him, share more, but I didn't. It would be too much like before, all about me.

"I was thinking we should take a drive up to the museum again," I said, suddenly. I hadn't meant to say it; the invitation could easily turn into a "should."

"That would be wonderful," he said without hesitation.

By then 40 minutes had passed. The big church around us was growing dim in the early evening. Dust-laden shafts of light shifted through the stained glass. We sat, quiet, the stillness thick and peaceful.

"I should get going," I said, rising slowly, knowing I would get an additional 15 minutes of gardening talk from him in the front of the church, partly just to talk to someone, and partly to keep me, his friend, there with him.

Outside, the grounds looked carefully cared-for with that same sort of order that Robert projected with his carefully trimmed beard, or his pants held high and tight with a belt. The evening was warm, with a peachy, early spring sky. Robert pointed up suddenly as a white egret flew straight and fast directly over us, its pointed ballet feet close and curved together like the eye of a needle. The sight was a surprise of pleasure for both of us. We turned and grabbed each other by the forearms, laughing.

"This is my Son, in whom I am well-pleased!" I exclaimed. "Revealed not with a dove, but an egret!"

Eighty

His visits over these years were marked by his birthday in February, Holy Week, and Thanksgiving. Several times, the

Super Bowl was a welcome distraction. I always forgot how much Robert knew about football and had enjoyed his time as a quarterback in high school. Each year I would note his upcoming birthday: 76, 77, 78, 79.

In 2013, on the day before Robert's 80th birthday party at our house, a major blizzard shut down the interstate. When I-95 opened again, John made it to church and picked up Robert and Fr. Tom; then they dug out another friend and brought her to our house. I made my way through the snow to pick up Clara nearby at the university. A couple of other neighbors came over and we ate chili and salad, drank a lot of wine, and with great amusement sang a song we had composed about him to the tune of "Downtown." After cake we cajoled him to read aloud Kinnell's poem "St. Francis and the Sow," and then someone else read "Little Sheep's Head Sprouting in the Moonlight," one of Robert's favorite poems in *The Book of Nightmares*:

> If one day it happens
> you find yourself with someone you love
> in a café at one end
> of the Pont Mirabeau, at the zinc bar
> where white wine stands in upward opening
>   glasses,
>
> and if you commit then, as we did, the error
> of thinking,
> one day all this will only be memory,
>
> learn,
> as you stand
> at this end of the bridge which arcs
> from love, you think, into enduring love,

learn to reach deeper
into the sorrows
to come—to touch
the almost imaginary bones
under the face, to hear under the laughter
the wind crying across the black stones. Kiss
the mouth
which tells you, here,
here is the world. This mouth. This laughter.
  These temple bones.

The still undanced cadence of vanishing.

Here, here is the world, I thought. It hadn't vanished yet. Although he didn't smile much, Robert went along with our wine-and-blizzard-induced hysteria and seemed to enjoy the celebration. It was unclear how much of these gatherings he took in. His lack of response may have been, more and more, simply not knowing what was going on.

Eighty. We would "reach deeper into the sorrows to come," but not that night. When I think of Robert on that birthday, I see him wearing the crazy Mardi Gras mask that one of the neighbors had bought him, and how strangely natural it looked on him over the usual blue parka that he wore all the time in the winter, indoors and outdoors.

No More Pruning

Sometime in 2013 Robert stopped officially working at St. James, put out by the many small requests he felt staff were making of him. The primary reason, though, was that Marcy, the office manager at St. James, told him he could no longer go up ladders to prune the trees. He was angry about this; it took a whole year for his complaints about this prohibition to ebb.

I wondered how not working would affect him, but Robert was very adamant about quitting. What did he do all day? He had never had a television or computer, and it seemed like he was reading less and less, hardly even pulling out his glasses. After an incident on Good Friday, when he fainted at the lectern while reading for Stations of the Cross and ended up breaking two ribs, he had stopped being a lector. His voice, unused, had become very soft and gravelly. We had been through a few cell phones, lost or overcharged, or too difficult to deal with. He didn't answer the phone often (was his hearing going?), and could not understand how to retrieve voice mail, so our communication was raggedy. He rarely called us.

After he quit the job, Robert continued to stop by the church most every day to putter around, assist in decorating or moving things for services, straighten up the hymnals and pick up bits of paper and trash after mass. Marcy kept tabs on him. She is a soul-and-a-half—kind, steady, humorous, realistic. Like many of the St. James parishioners, Marcy loved Robert for his "gentle, rigid quirkiness" and the way he was always trying to help others. While his repeated stories of about how he assisted this person or that always sounded defensive to me, like he was proving his worth, Marcy was a witness to the way that Robert took time to listen to people's stories, help load a car with groceries from the parish food bank, or find a missing purse in a pew.

Staff who worked at the Parish Center occasionally saw Robert's dark and angry side, too, but since he turned down all invitations to have coffee or dinner, no one knew much about what he did when he was not at church, or anything about his previous life. After he quit working at the church and was just stopping in, sometimes joining Marcy and others for lunch, Robert shared more about himself, how he had lived in San Francisco, the coyotes he raised in Colorado, his love of opera. He was a surprising story, unfolding.

An Afternoon in the Bronx

We still had some fine days with each other. One Friday I took the day off and we visited the New York Botanical Gardens, an exhibit of the "Gardens of the Alhambra," with cypress, olive, lemon and lime trees, all kinds of herbs and fountains, accompanied by several short poems by Federico Garcia Lorca posted throughout the outside gardens. I read the poems aloud as Robert and I wandered. We ate lunch in the café, then strolled some more among the conifers and the rock garden and had an easy drive home. I put music on, which broke the need to generate conversation. This was a better way to be with him, almost completely without expectations except the very basic ones of walking together. No need to tell him all of anything, or to listen for hours to his all-of-everything.

Our next adventure was an attempt to go to the Natural History Museum. I had mailed Robert printouts of the exhibits to look at since there was so much to see. Halfway there, on the Cross Bronx Expressway, the engine-overheat light in my car went on. That particular stretch was my idea of American highway hell, hot and muggy in the midday summer sun and usually stalled with huge trucks and irritable, aggressive drivers. "Not a place you'd want to break down," I had just said before the needle on my dashboard started to move to the red zone.

I managed to get off the Expressway, pull into a gas station, and park so the car could cool off. Across the street garish banner signs of four businesses ran into each other: car radio repair, ceramic tiles, alternator/air conditioning service, and auto glass. Three men were hanging around listlessly, two in folding chairs and one lounging against the building, waiting for business.

Although he was quite calm and wanted to be helpful, I knew Robert would be no help. While he looked through the car manual for the section on overheating, I walked over to the air conditioner shop. The owner, Juan, the only one who spoke English, told me to pull the car in. He tested the fuses and determined that the fan assembly was not working, which was causing the car to overheat. He assured me it was not a complicated issue and he could fix it. It would take maybe two hours and cost about $600—in cash. Juan seemed like a straightforward, friendly person, but the fact that he could work on the car immediately and was willing to drive me to the bank for the cash made me suspicious. A bad scenario was forming in my mind. What if they just needed work, as it seemed all the shops did, and were saying that they knew what was wrong but didn't? Then I would be paying cash, spending the whole day, and heading back home on the same Devil's Highway with the possibility—even likelihood—of overheating again. But what choice did I have? Call for a tow truck and take the car back to Connecticut? It would still have to be fixed.

So instead of going to the Museum, Robert and I spent the next four hours on the small side street along East 175th and Webster, watching the cars go in and out of the gas station, mechanics coming and going, picking up refurbished alternators from Juan's shop, an occasional customer at the radio shop. The day was hot, and it was not a neighborhood in which to go exploring. I went across the street and bought some donuts and coffee. Juan pulled out a couple of rickety fold-out chairs for us to sit in.

The radio guys alternated turns spraying down the pavement in front of their shop to cool off, occasionally dousing a car as it waited for the light. Every hour, a police car cruised slowly around the block. A Hispanic woman and her friend pulled up, looking to get their air conditioner charged. "Do you work here?" she asked. I was amused and flattered that she'd think the *gringa* in gray linen pants and a black t-shirt with sensible walking shoes, sitting alongside an elderly gentleman with a strange, inside-out T-shirt, suspenders, and black cargo pants would be running an alternator refurbishing shop.

Inside the garage, Juan and his nephew, who looked a lot like him, put the car up on the lift and struggled to get the fan assembly out. Then his nephew drove us in a beat-up Toyota to a bank about a mile away. The hot streets were chaotic, with crowds of people about, children in tow, doing business or waiting for business, unloading and loading appliances, mattresses. Street vendors selling fruit and vegetables and sunglasses. Two women shuffled up the street, one pushing an air tank for her emphysema while smoking a cigarette. The bank teller gave me my cash from behind ceiling-high bullet-proof glass.

Back at the shop, the first fan assembly that arrived was warped and Juan had to send it back. He showed it to me to prove it. "Won't work," he said. "Have patience. I will fix this well for you."

Having surrendered to the day and the heat, my anxiety changed to the patience Juan recommended. Robert and I could be in Ecuador, or Mexico. We were out of place, but we were in place. As a contrast to the nightmare I had imagined in the morning, my mind now generated a short list of things to be grateful for: I had been able to get off the highway; it was daytime; it hadn't been an accident, just a breakdown; there was a bathroom I could use; Juan was friendly even if I wasn't sure he could fix the car; I had the money to pay for the repair; Robert was with me to enjoy the strangeness of our experience and he, too, seemed filled with patience. I made him drink some water. We sat and watched the street and grew more comfortable. Big puffy summer clouds came and went overhead. Juan's wife came and retrieved the Toyota to pick up their toddler from daycare. Juan chatted with us a little. He was from Mexico City; he and his brother had two other shops within a mile from this one, which he'd had for two years. It was hard to make enough money, he said.

Juan fixed the car, and we were on our way back to Connecticut by later afternoon, exiting the Friday night rush traffic to eat at a diner outside Stamford. We had spent our day in the living museum of the Bronx. A strange day, but a fine one.

Fucking Narcissists

When was I going to be doing the poetry reading at the library? Robert wanted to know.

"What do you mean?" I asked.

"I understood that you were going to be reading there."

"Nope." The word "understood" usually meant that he had heard one of Them saying something.

"Well, you should go down there and tell them that you want to give a reading, and what dates you're available. And tell them there will be a lot of people coming."

"Hmm, Robert, it doesn't work that way. They invite you. You don't tell them when you're coming. I'm not even sure that would be something I'd want to do."

"Why do you say that?"

I didn't answer, not having it in me at that moment to get into a conversation about what dreams of his—of ours—had never come to fruition. I thought, also, of my poem that had recently been published. A couple of weeks earlier I had shown

Robert the magazine and pointed out the poem for him to read. He pored over it for a few moments but said nothing. Later I realized he did not understand any of it, or that I had written it. I didn't mind. We were moving past that stuff now.

"Nevertheless," he continued, "You should go to the library and make arrangements. Many people will come."

I looked at his somber, knowing face, and all the years of our desiring this and that. "Oh, Robert!" I exclaimed suddenly, "We're such fucking narcissists, you and I!"

I think he understood. Or at least he understood the tone of truth and ridiculousness and took relief in it. We looked at each other and laughed.

Mattapoisett

In the summer John and I decided to take Robert to John's brother's house in Mattapoisett, Massachusetts, for a couple of days for a little vacation while his brother was away. They drove up in the morning and I followed after work. We ate lobster and corn on the cob on the patio. Robert looked at the lobster blankly and said he didn't think he had ever eaten it before. We showed him how to crack the shell and fork out the meat. He was quiet and morose. After dinner, we passed around a book of Charles Wright's poems to each other for an impromptu reading. The poetry, with its fulsome, long-lined language, descriptions of landscapes and time passing, seemed right for the evening as the sun went down.

Robert examined the pages for perhaps 10 minutes, unable to find something to read, but possessive of the book. John and I cleaned up the dinner dishes. Later, inside, John and I made conversation, to entertain Robert, which, I realized, is what we had been doing for many years.

I picked a Wright poem for him, "Buffalo Yoga Coda III," about lying outside with the sun on his cheek. Robert read, his eloquent voice now gravelly, a beauty in the weakness of it. "That is very good," he commented.

Upstairs, even after a tour of the house, he was disoriented. I told him we would leave the bathroom light on. I noticed that he went to bed without washing or brushing his teeth. John said he had brought no normal things to take on a weekend away, such as extra clothes or books, just a jacket and some underwear and his toothbrush and some plastic bags in an insulated grocery bag. Robert had told us he was taking Benadryl to help him sleep—in the morning, at noon, and at night. He talked about taking "some other pills" but could not tell us what for. I never saw him take a pill. John and I let the topic go.

Robert was so out of it—I felt nervous being away with him. What if he had an episode?

In the morning he was better, going from room to room enjoying, as I did, the antiques and the light in the beautiful old New England house. I had to leave the next morning, but John and Robert stayed on another day, and he loosened up considerably. They found a plastic golf set that belonged to the grandchildren, and they putted about the large yard, chasing balls into the bushes.

John said Robert had told him, "It's so nice to be away," he said. "I don't have a home; it's nice to be in a home." Even second-hand, the remark stung, as if it was our fault Robert did not have a home. Who could make him a home, with room for all those voices? Not me.

Forgive me, forgive me.

Slippages

At Easter, he was silent in his usual holiday spot at the end of the table amidst the laughter and talk, poking and stirring his mashed potatoes, but not getting the fork to his mouth very often. Robert could use a resurrection, I thought; we all could. After dinner he fell asleep in his chair.

When I mentioned that he badly needed a haircut, Robert told me that the barber at his usual shop had told him to leave, "out of nowhere, for no reason whatsoever." At first I took the statement at face value, and then it occurred to me that he had had a delusional episode and scared the owner.

One day when I went to pick him up, Robert was in front of his building waiting, wearing the familiar dirty black pants, a blue long-sleeve shirt topped by a green short-sleeve shirt and fleece vest, with a woolen turtleneck sweater over his shoulder. Dressing in layers, I thought, almost amused, glad in any case not to see the perennial jacket with the pockets stuffed to bursting. Then I noticed he had shaved off his beard. It was the first time I had ever seen him without a beard, his lips so full above the small chin. He looked like a stranger. There were patches of whiskers on both cheeks, and I had the feeling the shaving was not intentional. Perhaps he had shaved too much in one spot and then had to continue with the whole beard. When I asked him about it, he ignored the question. Or maybe he didn't hear me, but I wasn't going to embarrass him by inquiring about that, either. We had probably assumed he was following the conversation a lot more than he was these past couple of years. He was such a good actor.

When I saw him now there were many slippages, conversations that started one place and meandered to another, usually to nature and the way he used to trim the trees, bringing the branches down toward him, rather than climbing up. When he talked he was almost completely in his own world, so sometimes we would ask a neighbor to join us for dinner, or other friends from church, to help shift the conversation and enliven the evening. Robert then seemed eager to talk, and others were glad to hear him. He talked of his childhood, or of things he "always did" in San Francisco, pulling together fragments of things that happened, or might have happened, or that he had read and turned into a story that happened to him. The stories evolved, got "mythological," as John said.

Robert told us he had been having "an issue," which we eventually concluded was incontinence—he wouldn't say it—and Marcy helped him schedule an appointment with a urologist she knew. John took him to the first appointment. "You should go in with him to see what's going on," I told him, but John felt that was too intrusive. The urologist gave Robert a prescription to try. On the day of the follow-up appointment Robert got lost and drove around Bridgeport for four hours. He didn't have his phone with him so couldn't call anyone.

"The street signs are completely incomprehensible!" he said angrily when he called me that evening. There was no point in arguing with him about it.

I bought him some Depends, calling them "special underwear," explaining how they worked. "Wouldn't it be easier just to use them?" I said, "Then you don't have to worry about it. You can go out and not worry about it. Millions of people do." But he wouldn't use them.

When we went to pick him up for Thanksgiving dinner, Robert came down and said he was sick, that he "hurt all over." He did not have a fever. What was pain to him? He said he wasn't sleeping—was it the voices, or the incontinence, or perhaps a urinary tract infection?

The next time I spoke to him, Robert said the "problem" had gone away, and he could now "last" for two hours. Obviously something should be done, but it was confusing, and it would require Robert acknowledging a problem and allowing someone to help him.

When Robert got to the point where he couldn't function, John said, we would find out, somehow, and help him more, if he would let us.

Bad Directions

Robert never exactly told us he was uncomfortable driving in the dark. "It will be quite late when I get home," he said a few times when we invited him over for dinner, or "The highway construction is so awful these days." Gradually, instead of him driving to our house I began to pick him up occasionally after work and bring him to our house to get him out of his apartment, hoping for an easy, low-key dinner, chat, maybe a movie. John drove him home.

One time when I came to get him he wasn't outside waiting. I called eight times with no answer. I was about to park and go up to his apartment to knock on the door, feeling nervous about what I might find, when he called. He said he thought dinner was the day before; he had waited for me, and I didn't come.

"Why didn't you just call me?" I said, exasperated. He didn't answer.

"I just have to get dressed," he said. It was 5 p.m.

When he came down to the car I told him to call me if he thought I was supposed to be there and didn't arrive. "Then you won't wonder, and I won't worry." (Although I did worry anyway.)

He was confused on a regular basis. I didn't need a doctor to explain. It was dementia: I said it to myself, finally. We were so slow to acknowledge it, just as we had been about his delusions.

Another night soon after, around 9 p.m., a friendly male voice left a message on my phone requesting that if I knew a Robert Proctor would I please call him—I did—and five minutes later a young man and his wife escorted Robert in his car to our house.

Robert had gotten lost going home from St. James, went too far, and ended up in the East End of Bridgeport, an easy place to become disoriented, especially at night. "If you don't stay to the left when you get off the highway, you're sunk," he said, frustrated and embarrassed. At our kitchen table, Robert moved the beach stones around as he described where he thought he went wrong in getting home. I was not able to picture the location.

By the fourth repetition of the story, he was weeping. I sat across from him, quiet. The space between us was very open and sad as I saw him taking in the information—finally, it seemed—that part of his mind was not working so well. After being so angry at all the people who gave him "wrong directions" when he had gotten lost recently, I was glad this time he wasn't blaming others.

I put my hand on his. "I can see that this is very hard for you," I said. I told him he needed to take his phone with him all the time. John drove Robert home in his car that night and I followed. When he didn't answer our calls the following two days, John went over. Although Robert let him into the apartment, John said he'd "gone off" again. There were now "little people" outside his window; the police recently arrested several of them, he said. It was not Robert's fault that he had confused directions; They were messing with the street signs.

"Robert, we've been down this path before," John said to him.

"You don't believe me, but it is true."

"I know it's true for you, but it's not happening in the regular world. Things are getting harder for you; you're losing some of your cognitive abilities—you're 83, for godsakes! It's going to happen to all of us. The question is, how are you going to deal with it?"

Robert scoffed.

"Well, we're here for you."

John called him again the next day, with no answer. We then had a "Robert talk" and I concluded, "Well, he's not living with us."

John shrugged. "It could go that way."

"No, he can't live with us. We already tried that, remember? He was messed up in a big way even when he was with us."

When Robert was in Delusion Land, just thinking of him was a drain. We had become caregivers, and that was that.

"If you want him to live here, I'll tell you what—he can live here and I'll go to his place!" I exclaimed.

John rolled his eyes at me. At the end of the week he drove over to Robert's. A resident let him into the building and he knocked on Robert's apartment door until Robert finally opened it a crack and peered out. When he saw John he scowled and told him to go away.

"'Get out of here!' is what he said. He thinks I'm one of Them," John said, perturbed. It was odd to see him unsettled. "There's nothing I can say to convince him otherwise, probably." He paused. "I hate to admit it—I'm a little relieved. I don't want to see him like that." Another pause. "But I know it rests on you, then." An apology hung in the air between us. "I'll help you however I can," he said, finally.

"What are we going to do?" I asked, the question joining the apology. I was asking myself this constantly, but not out loud. We were together, but I was alone.

I Get the Job Done

Not long afterward, Robert decided finally that his car was no longer functional. As usual, I took his statement at face value and offered to have the car checked out by our mechanic. "He won't be able to fix it," Robert said. "It's not fix-able." They had ruined the car, he said; he could no longer drive it. We let the subject drop. Obviously, and probably luckily, he had decided not to drive anymore, for fear of getting lost. He gave me the keys. I discovered that his registration and his driver's license were both expired.

Since he wasn't driving, Marcy began picking him up midday on Tuesdays and Fridays and bringing him to the Parish Center. She offered him lunch—whatever she and anyone else who was around was eating—and then put him to work shredding documents with the huge, old shredder. It was a far cry from the gardening and landscaping he used to do, but it occupied his time and the setting was familiar.

At first he shredded church documents—old tax documents, checks, correspondence—then Marcy brought in some personal documents from home to shred. Eventually she gave Robert junk mail to rip up—magazines, old catalogs, anything at hand to keep him busy. He would spend the afternoon feeding the machine, accumulating the remains in bags which he hauled to the recycling bin behind the church. Instead of talking about landscaping, now each time I saw him Robert described the shredding process—the stacks of paper he set up at various heights, the difficulties of inserting the right amount of paper into the machine, the huge bag the shredded pieces went into—demonstrating all this with long, skinny, eloquent arms.

"I save the church a lot of money," he said. "I get the job done." He repeated this a few times. I realized he had said this about every job he had had over the years. To be working and feel skilled at the work at hand was important to him. But I knew from Marcy that the shredding job had become less do-able. Robert was confused, and less steady on his feet. She continued to pick him up a couple of times a week, just to get him out to have lunch with her and other staff who knew him.

One evening she called to tell me that Robert had walked the two and a half miles from his apartment to church in the midday August heat. When he arrived at the empty church, he was disoriented and exhausted, sweating profusely.

"The Bishop is supposed to be here this evening," he told the woman who happened to be leaving the Parish Center. "I was told to walk here, not to drive."

He continued with this story, frustrated that the church was empty and there was no event. The woman tried to take him home, but Robert was unable to tell her exactly how to get there and had her drop him off at the cemetery not far from his apartment building. John drove to his apartment that night to confirm that he had gotten home. Robert answered the door but would not let John in or speak to him—he was still angry from their last conversation—but John could see he was okay.

I called the Area Agency on Aging to see what could be done, and they said Robert might qualify for companion or home health aide services, or delivered meals, but he would have to see a doctor for a physical and, of course, be agreeable to the idea. I did not see how that was going to happen if he wouldn't let anyone besides me into his apartment, and a physical would be of no use without an interpreter to go with him.

Since he wouldn't speak to John, I was checking in with him regularly now, when and if he answered the phone. He sounded upbeat—or was it manic?—as I listened. He said he had been getting better sleep now that the cops had arrested some of the people, including those people who made him fall down at church and break his ribs. He was blaming Them for everything.

196

"I know you two don't believe it," he said.

The conversation about our disbelief continued over the next few weeks. Several Saturday afternoons I picked Robert up to go to Mass and afterward took him to Stationhouse, a restaurant near church. We would sit at the bar, where we could be companionable but not have to talk. There was an easy normalcy about the place. Every half hour or so a Metro-North train pulled in, and from our perches we could see the platform and the legs of passengers entering and exiting the train. Usually there was baseball or hockey on the TV screen behind the bar, and the regulars at the bar provided good people-watching. We were almost regulars ourselves, I thought. Robert would have a bowl of chili and I'd order sushi.

"I get along well with people," he was saying to me sternly. "I am not 'cuckoo' or a 'lunatic' or 'crazy'. I'm not!" That evening he did, however, look like a street person, with his uncut hair, unkempt beard, dirty jacket, and that fluorescent orange knit cap he was so fond of.

"I've never called you crazy. Those are the wrong words," I replied. "What you are experiencing is true for you. And its impact is certainly true for me." The statement was now a clinical refrain.

"I am telling you. It is true! It is happening!" Robert banged his palm on the edge of the bar and a couple of customers glanced over at us.

He paused and looked sharply at me. "You don't call anymore. We never do anything. It has been a long, long time since we did anything."

The accusation made my heart jump to my throat. "No, it hasn't been a long time. I see you at least every other week. We come here to the bar. We go to church. You come to the house when you let yourself. I do call. *You* could call, for once!" Now I was on the edge of yelling at him.

He sat on the bar stool, ridiculous in his jacket and hat in the warm weather, the usual look of arrogance and defense. Of course he couldn't call; he probably no longer remembered how to.

"Robert," I said suddenly, another rogue wave of anger rising, "Do you remember when I came to San Francisco to get you? Do you remember? You were going down. For the same reason as now you were totally going down, and you probably would have died if I hadn't come to get you." By then I had tears in my eyes and was about to slam *my* hand on the edge of the bar.

Seeing my emotion quieted him. And then someone on the screen over the bar hit a home run, and we were both, thankfully, taken out of ourselves. A song played in the background: "Wild, wild horses…couldn't drag me away…" He put his hand out and I took it.

Once one of the regulars at the bar asked Robert and me if we were a couple. Maybe it was the way Robert often reached out for my hand—not fatherly. "We're good friends," I told the woman.

NAMI

"Have you been to a NAMI meeting? It might help. You should go." Friends whose daughter had schizophrenia had found support in the regular meetings at the National Alliance on Mental Illness. I wanted to find a strategy to get Robert to a doctor, so we could get some help—perhaps a companion or home health aide—maybe even some psychiatric help.

I went to the monthly support group at a nearby church. There were about 20 of us, mostly couples. I was the only new person, and as we went around the room sharing our latest stories and incidents what I noticed most was the dark-humor camaraderie among them. There was very little commentary, just focused listening and sympathetic nods. Most were parents of young adults with a mental illness—schizophrenia, primarily. One couple's 19-year-old daughter had tried to drive into her mother with the family car. Another reported on how worried they had been about their 25-year-old son going into the city on his own. The leaders of the group said how grateful they were that their son was stable for the time being, especially since it had only been a few months since he came at his father with a butcher knife.

An elderly woman, quite nervous, told the group that she lived alone with her husband of 50 years. He was acting more and more strange and she didn't know what to do. Recently, in a sudden fit of anger, he had threatened to drive them both off the road. Hers was the only story where the leaders offered advice, asking her if she had a plan. Was there a place she could go when her husband got like that?

Another couple queried the group about a psychiatrist who had been recommended for their daughter. "Can I be blunt here?" one woman answered. "Go anywhere else than that place. It's just a medication factory. That's all they do."

When they got to me, I almost took a pass. Why had I come here, again? Robert's situation seemed so tame. It was only a delusional disorder; he wasn't violent, even when he was angry. And—oh thank God—he wasn't my teenage son.

A Little Late

He was in rough shape again in the front of his building, no coat in the cold morning air, his hair uncombed, trying not to cry. He'd lost his debit card (he couldn't remember what to call it) and his other cards—he'd been looking for them everywhere—so I parked and went all the way into his apartment with him for the first time in many years. The furniture was strangely arranged, bookcases facing each other, a hollow-core door placed on top of the kitchen table for a desk, and most surfaces piled with newspapers and church bulletins. The kitchen was dusty but clean, unused. The build-up was not as bad as the San Francisco apartment 12 years ago, but I could see it wouldn't be long until it was.

After going through several plastic bags, I suggested he check his pants pockets one more time, and the small plastic packet of cards was there, a relief for both of us. Then we drove to our house, had some lunch, and put his laundry in the washer. He calmed down more and more until he was almost his regular self, and we both relaxed. Before dinner, we took a slow walk in the short woods before dinner and watched a light shower of big fat snowflakes in the afternoon sun. With his thin white hair, he seemed like a snowflake himself—delicate, unique.

The next morning he called very early and left a message that he couldn't find his cards again. His words were slurry and he sounded distraught. When I called him back, he had found them.

His confusions were increasing. "He wouldn't do well in a facility," Fr. Tom said when I talked to him about the situation. "He needs to stay in his apartment as long as possible." Although, I thought, in a "facility" they could probably monitor and assure that he took medication, and then maybe the voices would go away. But, realistically, it was probably a little late for that.

In the Foxhole
2017

In the fall of 2016, Robert told me that he wanted to clear out his books and give them away. I said I would help him if he liked, knowing that it would be much more than clearing out books. When she heard about his plan, Marcy offered to help.

I was glad to have a partner. We arrived early at Robert's building. I had coffee for us and an egg sandwich for him, as well as trash bags, new boxes, and cleaning supplies. Neither of us could reach him by phone; he was sleeping hard. He didn't answer the buzzer either, so Marcy and I sat on the floor in the foyer, drank our coffee and talked for about 15 minutes while waiting for someone to come and unlock the door. I told her that his apartment probably was not as bad as it had been, but to be prepared.

Robert finally answered the door, just waking up, wearing a shirt and some huge oversize boxers that he was holding up with one hand. Marcy and I cheerfully made our way in, acting as if all was normal, and gradually Robert remembered that we had planned to come over. He got dressed and brushed his teeth in the kitchen sink while we assessed the situation. The heat was on high; it was sweltering in the apartment. I lowered the temperature and asked permission to open the blinds and windows to cool the place down. Robert drank the coffee and ate the egg sandwich and after about 15 minutes, with food in him, he was more himself and we all continued in our calm-and-normal act.

I put on some music with my iPod and portable speaker and we began our work. Marcy and Robert sorted through his clothes. Usually Marcy was directing Robert's tasks when he came to volunteer at the Parish Center. "So now you get to tell *me* what to do," she said to him. I took on the main room, filling bag after bag with trash that had piled up over the past 12 years, thinking of the clean-up of his apartment in San Francisco. As before: folded paper towels, plastic bags, newspapers and miscellaneous articles, magazines, *Magnificats* with their daily scripture readings and reflections. Twisties for plastic bags, carefully arranged in a paper cup. The mail was mostly from Catholic Relief Services, the Diocese, St. James, People's Bank, Allstate (old), Wells Fargo (old), and me. Christmas cards, birthday cards, cards with bookmarks and photos—my handwriting all over. I *have* tried to reach him, I told myself as I threw these cards into a bag.

Garden and winter gloves, mostly new, were stuffed in the bookshelves like hands waiting to be held. Brand new garden tools in the closet. A heart monitor, unopened and probably outdated. Old cell phone boxes and instructions. Expired calendars.

I was hoping to finish in one day—obviously impossible—so I just filled bag after bag, not contemplating much what to keep, talking cheerfully to Robert as he wandered in and out of the room, unable to help us.

"Go ahead," he said. "Just do it."

We had gotten rid of so many books in San Francisco that I was surprised at how many more he accumulated in 12 years. This time, however, they were beautiful books. Duplicates and sometimes triplicates of his favorites: Kinnell, of course, and Mary Oliver, W.S. Merwin, William Trevor. Other poets. This time there were also many spiritual books: St. Ignatius of Loyola, Thérèse of Lisieux, Karl Rahner. I stacked them on the floor; later Marcy began packing them into the many double-brown bags Robert had collected, and by late morning there were two long rows of bags in the front room.

I could see that several more cleaning days would be needed in order for me to feel comfortable visiting him here. That was what we were headed toward, I thought.

As we loaded the trash bags into the van, I could see Robert becoming serious and downtrodden from the stress of getting rid of so much and from having us in his apartment. "There are bad people," he said, looking up at the thruway overpass nearby, "and they make a lot of noise." He shook his head at me. "It's true."

"Yes, I know it's true for you," I said. "I don't hear them, but I know you do." The refrain.

We took the bags of trash to the dump, had lunch at the diner, and came to my house afterward to sign forms I had downloaded. Robert had agreed to create a Durable Power of Attorney, Advanced Health Directive, and a Will. "It'll make everything easier," I said. "I can pay your rent; you won't have to worry about it anymore." (I did not say that I could also accompany him to the doctor.) We had opened a joint bank account a couple of years before. "I want you to have access to everything," he had said. I didn't think much about it at the time, except it was probably a good idea and I was glad that it was his suggestion and not mine. Although he did not have a lot of money, I was surprised that he managed to save money while living on Social Security. He didn't buy anything anymore, no newspapers or coffee, and little food, just oranges and Clif bars and canned salmon at Trader Joe's.

Three of our neighbors, one of whom was a notary, came over to witness and notarize the signing. "Here," I pointed at each line for him to initial or sign on the many pages. Although it was somewhat serious, the talk among us as we sat around the kitchen table was relaxed and easy. They all knew Robert from the nine months he had lived with us and many family gatherings, such as Kevin and Clara's graduations. We toasted with a glass of wine afterward. Robert seemed relieved.

With the letting-go and handing-over, the day was almost sacramental. When I wasn't fighting myself about him or wishing he didn't have a mental illness or wasn't losing all his cognitive abilities, there was a lightness that opened up. I had been fighting and worrying and resisting for most of the time I had known him, just as he had been.

John and I brought all the books back to our house and for two weeks they filled our living room, 600 books stacked on the coffee table, the mantle, in front of the fireplace. I attempted to sort them into general piles: Philosophy, Fiction, Poetry, Religion, Other. We invited neighbors and friends to come and take their pick, although I put most of the poetry in a bookcase upstairs.

I had found cash in several of the books. On the day we had gone to clean up his apartment, Marcy had handed me, without comment, a book of poems by George Seferis. Pressed between the pages was a lock of my long, 18-year-old, reddish-brown hair, tied with a piece of string. I did not remember giving it to him, but I must have.

There was a weight in all this. "You're probably relieved," said a friend from church.

"Relieved?"

"Relieved that you've made your decision—you're going to take care of him."

There were the signed, notarized papers. And so I was going to take care of him, again. But it was not a relief; it was a definitive burden; I felt it and realized I'd had very few burdens in my life, really, and none like this chosen one.

I spoke to Fr. Tom often about the situation. "You're in the foxhole now," he said to me. "Now you hunker down. Keep your head down when the bullets are flying. Don't stand up or you'll get shot."

I was coming by his apartment regularly after work to take Robert to get his few groceries and then to Panera for some soup and bread. He paced strangely outside my car, and as we crossed the parking lot he told me They had made him piss his pants. I said we could get the food to go. In the restaurant I asked if he wanted to use the bathroom and he yelled at me, "That's not it—that had nothing to do with it!" I was stung but pulled myself together. He apologized profusely on the way home.

"Can I still come up and unload the groceries and eat supper?" I asked, finally, when we pulled into the parking lot.

"Of course."

As we waited for the elevator, he was pacing again, shaking his head angrily at something he was hearing, no longer able to pretend in front of me. I was frightened of him when he was like this. I wanted to say, "I'm here, too," but didn't.

In the apartment, it took him 40 minutes to undress and lay out his wet pants. I ate my soup, thinking that any questions or advice would be too much for him. He was in the bathroom with the light out. He finally came out in some huge boxers and said he couldn't find any damn pants and he couldn't get any light on in the room. I showed him where his clothes were, in the open bookcase, and the lamp on the other side of the bed. Finally, he sat down at the table and ate with me and I could visibly see him improving, coming-to, as he ate. He probably hadn't eaten since yesterday.

"The trouble I'm having can't be a physical malady," he continued, in his formal mode, "like some byproduct of being old. It is too inconsistent. I only have trouble when They bother me... Excuse me, please." As if on cue, he got up and made his way slowly to the bathroom.

A couple of minutes later he motioned to me to come. There was blood in the toilet. "See what they do to me!" he exclaimed. "Every damn day! They're coloring it."

"No, Robert, that's blood," I said in my calmest voice. "You need to see a doctor."

"No, it's not. It's not!"

"I'm not going to argue with you."

We returned to the living room and sat in the dim room. I was reluctant to turn on any light besides the hall light. Already I could feel our altercation in the bathroom fading, as if he had forgotten about it.

"Blood in the urine is serious, Robert. I don't see Them, but I did see that blood."

"You do not understand! There is nothing that can be done. They are ruining my life. It is completely unfair, unjust. You don't understand."

We were quiet a while. Then I said, "These voices are ruining your life. Maybe it's time to look into meds again." I paused, remembering what I'd read in *I'm Not Sick, I Don't Need Help* book, trying out the technique of offering a choice. "But what I think is not important. It's your call."

"What you think is important," Robert said.

"But not as important as what you think. It's your body, your mind."

Robert stroked his beard as he looked at me. "What do you suggest I do?"

"I don't know, R, but maybe it would be good to get a physical, in general, to check you out overall. I could help you and set that up."

"All right, then," he said.

Had he said "okay"? Success! I could search for a doctor.

Robert was looking at me in a pondering way. "I try and think of all this as if I were you, and I would have a hard time believing it, too. I guess I would. And I would try and sit and listen to you and try and help you."

He so rarely referred to me these days; I was touched.

As I watched him sip his soup in silence I looked around the room, trying not to think of the cleaning and tossing left to do, trying to relax and will the apartment to be friendly to him, to exorcise those demons that hung about him like an aura. The three rooms were mostly orderly now, but I somehow intuited that I was not to move any furniture. The only comfortable chair, which I was sitting in, I now understood to be placed in this odd corner alongside the kitchen because when he sat in it They couldn't see him. Two narrow bookcases faced each other with a small space between; I guessed he sometimes hid there from Them. Another bookcase was alongside the window to obscure the view. His jacket and clothes from the previous week were hung on the backs of the kitchen chairs. Although it was still not a comfortable place, there was nothing in it that felt menacing to me and I was grateful for that. I was often afraid Robert's demons would somehow leak out of him toward me. Instead, I experienced the residue of them.

If I were him, what would I see?

Oh, I couldn't think about this anymore! I had bought him a sweater and a fleece throw blanket. I'd ordered a "dementia clock," too, with a large, backlit display of day, date, and time of day (evening, afternoon, night, morning). I doubted he would use any of these items, and I resolved not to buy anything else for a while. My fix-it mode was not really that good for either one of us. I didn't want to leave him alone, but I could not bear to be with him. He was the one who was in the foxhole.

"I know it's very difficult for you, R," I said as I stood up to leave. I went over to his chair and he put his arms around my waist in a hug, like a child. "I'm going to find a doctor and make an appointment," I said. "I'm praying for you." I was. Each thought, even the angry ones, were like prayers. I needed them to be prayers, not curses. His spine protruded under my hand like that of someone starving. "Peace be with you," I said. It was all I could say.

"God bless you," he responded. He had taken to saying that most every time I saw him, or when he couldn't remember what else to say.

Now that he had agreed and I had Power of Attorney, I found him a doctor. I wrote Dr. M a letter, explaining Robert's delusions and his living situation so that at the appointment I would not have to explain it in front of Robert. As the three of us sat cramped in the small, fluorescent examining room, Robert watched the doctor skeptically as he scrolled through computer screens filling in information.

"So, Robert, is there any particular reason you're here today?"

"No."

"Robert," I said, "what about the blood in your urine?"

"I don't know about that."

"Can I tell the doctor about it?"

"Yes."

Dr. M was kind and took his time as he gave Robert a cursory check-up, giving us a referral to a urologist.

"This is my good friend, who takes care of me," Robert said, reaching out suddenly and clasping my hand. "We've known each other for a very long time."

"Everyone can use a good friend," Dr. M said.

The urologist confirmed a large malignant-cell tumor in Robert's bladder, probably Stage 4, but impossible to tell without a cystoscopy. Because of his age, this would probably mean a hospital procedure and overnight stay.

Marcy went with us to the oncologist. The doctor went on for a couple of minutes about the possibilities of treatment, how he would recommend removal of the bladder if Robert were younger, and how the chemotherapy for bladder cancer was still very potent and difficult to go through. But there were other things they could do. What did Robert think?

Robert looked at him. "I don't know quite what to think."

The oncologist looked at us, finally taking in Robert's non-comprehension.

"What if we do nothing?" Marcy asked him.

"That's an option, too."

After a month, I stopped trying to explain to Robert that he had bladder cancer. Except for having to urinate frequently, and the blood, he had no other symptoms. I gave his car away to the maintenance man and let the building manager know that I was Robert's Power of Attorney and would be checking on him. I introduced myself to the other residents, who told me that they had seen a deterioration in Robert, especially over the past few months. He had been seen wandering late at night. One morning at 1 a.m. he pulled the fire alarm in the hallway and a fire truck came, waking most of the residents.

"The sign said, 'Pull for Help,'" Robert said to me the next day. "I was locked out of my apartment. I needed help."

I laughed; he did not.

Throughout this disintegration, he maintained his professorial air of calm, measured authority, even when what he said made little sense. When I would point something out to him, he would disagree.

"The way you are talking, it sounds like I have a serious medical condition," he repeated to me.

"You do, Robert. You've got bladder cancer."

He stroked his beard, picking at the scrambled eggs and spinach I had made for him. "I would know if I did. I would have symptoms."

"You do have symptoms. You've lost about 8 pounds in the past month, and you have blood in your urine."

"I don't know about that," he said doubtfully.

Our conversations would circle around like that. I felt closer to him now when we didn't talk, and I preferred getting out of the apartment and going to the Stationhouse after Saturday Mass, where he would lighten up after a glass of wine, and the bar TV and hum around us would hold us in a kind of embrace. "He should have had that," Robert would cluck at a bad play in the baseball game on TV, and I was simply glad that he seemed able to follow the game.

Marcy and I were now in an alternating routine of stopping at his apartment most every day to check on him, reporting back to each other on Robert's state of being like professional case managers. We noticed that he did not eat except when we came with lunch or took him to breakfast, nor would he eat any of the prepared food we left in the refrigerator. He could not comprehend the microwave or coffeemaker (I had found a new one in his closet), and eventually he stopped using the toaster, too. The stove, clean and pristine, had not been used in a long time.

We took in these details, day by day, week by week. It was surprising how quickly we became accustomed to the diminishment of his capabilities. I depended on Marcy, whose parents and in-laws had all had long demises, for feedback and guidance. Except for John's father, I had had little caregiving experience. My mother and father were in their 80s, living separately, mostly healthy and independent. It had been relatively easy to care for John's father when we had first moved to Connecticut. Ed had been easygoing. His illnesses were managed, and not mental; his family was nearby to help at any time. Robert's mental illness was a sealed metal box I carried around with Marcy's help.

One day I got a call from the building manager that Robert had left the building and was pacing outside with a bag of some sort. He said he was waiting for a ride. When Marcy came to visit three hours later, she found Robert still outside, wearing another oddly layered outfit, a laundry bag of dirty clothes slung over his shoulder. He ignored her at first, obviously frustrated.

"Hi, Robert. It's Marcy."

"I know who you are!"

"What are you doing out here?"

"I've been waiting a long time. For some friends. They are picking me up and we are going to spend a few days at a lovely home."

"Why don't we go inside and get some food?" she suggested.

It was Mattapoisett he was thinking of, I told her when she recounted what had happened. Would there be some way to take him there again? I wondered. In his apartment I had recently found a handwritten note on the back of a large envelope:

Clark Institute

3 Trips: a great time each visit. We spent most of each day, and each of us liked several different paintings and displays. I hope someday that for the heck of it we will look again. For us for the paintings for the joy of a day; for the happiness!!

He liked that old phrase, "for the heck of it," and said it when he was happy. Would there be a way to take him to the Clark again? If we didn't have to take care of his daily needs, perhaps these trips would be possible, but not in this grind.

"I think maybe we should tell R that we will not take him out if he doesn't take a shower," Marcy emailed one day. Robert had not taken a shower in at least two months. He didn't smell, but his hair was greasy.

"I do that," he scoffed when I suggested I help him take a shower. "In there, all the time." He pointed to the bathroom, but it was hard to tell what he meant, as it was, increasingly, about everything.

Finally, one Friday a couple of weeks later I surprised him after work with a bottle of wine and some supper, and after we had each had a glass of wine I said, "So, Robert, how about I help you take a shower?"

He looked sheepish. "Okay."

Yes! I thought. We were going to do this! I was energized in my Competent Way.

I had always thought of him as modest, but Robert had no hesitation about getting undressed in front of me. "It'll be easier if you sit down on the bed," I said, and directed him while he took off his pants and shorts. I willed myself not to be shocked at how thin he was, how fragile and dry his skin was, hanging on his bones, as the cliché went. I turned on the heater in the bathroom, got the water just right, had him test it, and helped him to get into the tub and sit down on the built-in folding seat, feeling grateful for the handicap-accessibility.

"This feels very good," he repeated several times, soaping himself with the washcloth I gave him as I ran the warm water over him with the flexible spout.

"That's the idea, feeling good," I said, teasing, but nervous. I knew there was a proper way to give a geriatric shower, but I did not know what it was. "Is it too hot?"

"It's fine, it's very good." For 20 minutes he enjoyed the water, and I enjoyed him enjoying it. I washed his hair with the baby shampoo I had bought, remembering bathing Kevin, and later Clara, squatting by the tub, holding their soft baby bodies steady with one hand as I poured water over them with the other.

When we were finished, Robert slipped as he stood up—not badly, but I could see from the fear on his face that he had probably fallen before, another reason he didn't want to take a shower, never mind the confusing, one-knob faucet. Getting out of the tub, he was very careful, taking my arm, naming each movement in advance like it was a complex gymnastics sequence. I guided him to the chair by the tub where we carefully dried off. I gave him a squirt of lotion and told him to rub it onto his arms.

"Those need attention," he said, pointing at his toenails, which were quite long. I found a trimmer in the cabinet and clipped them, and then his fingernails. How narrow and elegant, his feet and hands.

"Thank you very much," he repeated several times.

Clean clothes. More supper. A second glass of wine to celebrate our achievement.

But the memory of how good it was to take a shower would not stay with him, nor the memory of other conversations.

"The problem is," he said the next time I saw him, "is that you have it in your mind what I am and am not capable of. You have decided." He smiled at me in a challenging, aloof way.

He was right; I had decided. It was more and more obvious: he didn't know which car door to get into, how to get dressed, which food he was eating. And all around the country, hundreds of thousands of family and friends like me were caring for someone in this way, monitoring "ADL"s (Activities of Daily Living, which I had just read about, such as feeding oneself, bathing, dress, and toileting), putting in hours and hours of presence and decision-making and cajoling and explaining.

I wanted out. Out.

A few days after one of our negative conversations, when I came to see him, I found another note he had scrawled on a piece of notebook paper:

In my life where do I go?
How will I be able to live?
What will happen now?
Am I to be put away somewhere?
What have I dun?
Please help me!

His handwriting, with its mixed upper and lower-case letters and misspelling, startled me to tears.

I tried to talk to him about it, but he was unable to focus. "I am worried that I won't be able to get food," he said, finally.

"We will get you food," I replied. "You just have to remember to eat it." I knew Robert did not want to be "put away," as he had been as a child. But he was not making it easy.

Over the months I had run the scenarios over in my head of how Robert could possibly move in with us. Perhaps he could be in the sunporch, with easy access to the bathroom. Maybe if he lived with us we could demand he take medication for the delusions. And if he was on medication, maybe he would accept companions and home health aides during the day who could accompany him on walks, read books with him. And what about at night? Would he wander? What would our lives—John and mine—be like?

These speculations hit a full-stop as I remembered that over the nine months he did live with us our presence did not keep the voices at bay, nor did he do what we wanted him to. We talked about it over dinner. It was a brief conversation.

For six months, Marcy and I continued our routine. We knew we could not get him into a nursing home without some sort of emergency and proof he could not live on his own. We waited.

When the time came it did not feel like an emergency as much as something that simply had to be done. One Saturday I noticed a sheet in the garbage, and a stain on his mattress and the floor beside his bed, an accident that Robert had obviously tried to clean up. I made him the lunch I usually did—scrambled eggs with spinach and toast—and said nothing for a while. He did not seem to notice when I went in with a pot of steaming water to scrub the mattress and floor. When I finished I asked him how he was doing. "There was quite a mess in your bedroom," I said. "It looked like you had an accident. What happened?"

His look was blank. "I have no idea."

Later that afternoon in church he did not feel well again and admitted that this might have been going on for a few days. He wasn't sure. I remembered, also, that he did not drink water unless reminded to, and was probably getting dehydrated.

The next morning, one of his neighbors called to let me know that Robert had wandered out of the building and into the neighborhood. The police brought him back to the building. He was spiraling down.

Mission Critical

We had arrived at the hospital about 4:30; it was now approaching 6 p.m. and the summer sky outside the Emergency Room entrance was fading. After the intake, Robert reclined on his gurney as we waited in the hallway of the ER. Patients were lined up on the other rolling gurneys alongside the wall like planes waiting on a runway. Two of them also had companions with them. I acquired two blankets for Robert against the chill of the air conditioning, and we watched the Monday evening theatrics of the ER. Although several patients were brought in, no one had an immediate emergency, and so one by one they were lined up with us.

It had been a long afternoon getting him here. The day before Marcy had emailed me a gentle ultimatum: *I think we have hit mission critical. No matter how much push-back he gives, he can really no longer stay on his own… I am very worried that something bad is going to happen... I would be happy to be there with you to meet the nurse or whoever comes in to tell them that we need to move him to some sort of facility as soon as possible.*

I felt frightened, but as soon as she said it, I knew it was true. We could not keep going along as we had been.

I had called Dr. M, made an appointment, and left work midday. Robert came to the door when I knocked; he had clothes on, but he could barely shuffle across the room to get back to the couch. How had we gotten to this point? I knelt in front of him and took his hand. "Listen, I'm here to take you to the doctor. That's what we're going to do and I don't want to argue about it."

To my surprise, he nodded. I made him some eggs and toast, which revived him somewhat. At Dr. M's office I explained that Robert had been deteriorating, and had had a bout of diarrhea and hadn't been eating much—whatever I could think of to prompt the situation toward the hospital, knowing that once there they could not release him if he couldn't take care of himself. Dr. M was a little slow on understanding, and had suggested, again, home care, or an aide. "We've tried that," I reminded him. "He won't let anyone in. I think he needs some help now."

"The hospital?"

"Yes."

"When were you thinking?" The doctor looked at me, then at Robert. "Now?"

I nodded. "I think that would be a good idea."

Robert was calm throughout all this; it was impossible to tell what or if he was thinking. We drove to the hospital in silence.

Now, in the hospital hallway, it looked like we would be here for a while. I had helped him with a urine sample, which I gave to the nurse.

"Am I going to go back to where I was before?" he asked.

"Probably not." I thought of the note he had scrawled several weeks before.

"Where will I go?"

"We don't know yet. Somewhere you can get help anytime, and food. You can't live alone; you need more help."

He did not argue. He asked the question several more times over the next couple of hours. At 11 p.m. he was wheeled into an actual examining room, where the attending doctor tried to figure out why we were there. He asked Robert first, then me. I gave the same story. "He's having trouble on his own."

The doctor asked Robert what day it was, who the president was. "I'm unsure of that," Robert said.

"What is your name?"

"P-r-o-c-t-o-r," Robert spelled out his last name.

"Okay," the doctor said with a sigh, knowing that the social work department would have yet another placement case on their hands. "You've got a urinary tract infection, so we'll be admitting you. It'll take some time to get the room sorted out."

When he left, Robert seemed the calmest I'd seen him in a long time, and oddly alert.

"Where are we?" he asked.

"We're in the hospital," I repeated.

"If we're in the hospital I must have something seriously wrong with me."

"Yes. You have bladder cancer, and you have an infection right now."

"How long have I had this illness?" He was present, genuinely curious.

"I'm not sure. Maybe a year, or eight months. It started showing up with the blood in your urine, and I'm not sure when that started."

"Oh."

"You didn't want to believe that it was blood—you kept saying that those people whose voices you hear had done it to you."

A pause.

"You have a mental illness," I said.

"Do I?"

"Yes."

"How long has that been going on?"

"A long time. I don't know. Maybe 25 years, maybe longer." I paused. He was still listening intently. "I know it's been hard for you. And even harder because part of the illness is that you can't tell you have it—you can't believe it, no matter what happens."

Robert seemed to take this in.

"I've been lost," he said. His voice was soft and straightforward. "I've been lost. For a long while I've been confused. I haven't known what's been going on, and I've made decisions—confused decisions—that have messed up my life. For a long while."

Oh, my friend. For these 20 minutes in the ER he was the man I had known before. I wished I weren't so tired, so I could pay closer attention. We were quiet together. Outside I could hear the swish of hospital personnel up and down the corridor of examination rooms. A blue curtain blocked our view. The huge clock over the sink looked like it should tick, but it was silent.

"Did I ever hurt anyone?" he asked.

I thought of how he had slammed the door on John, and on our friend from St. James who had tried to help, and other parishioners, and of the many likely incidents with his neighbors in the apartment building—but he had never physically hurt anyone. "No, Robert. Never. You are gentle in your heart, even when you're angry."

"Was I ever mean to you?"

I shrugged. He reached for my hand. "Has this been difficult for you?" he asked.

I almost laughed. "Yes."

He took my hand. "I am so sorry, so sorry. Please forgive me." We gazed at each other. He was weeping.

"Of course I forgive you. Of course."

"Thank you. Thank you for everything."

When I left, finally, after midnight they still hadn't gotten a hospital bed, but would soon. "He's a sweetheart," one of the nurses said.

The nurses changed their tune after Robert was in the hospital for two days, finally moving him to a single room right off the nurses' station where they could monitor him. The second night, in a delusional state, he had gone into another patient's room and hit him with a pillow. He alternated between docile and awful for the week he was in the hospital and we awaited a nursing home placement. I met with a woman from hospice. He would have a team of a nurse and social worker checking in with him regularly, and Medicare would pay for it.

A place was found, the only place in the county that would take him, and it happened to be near our house. I tried to think of it as good fortune. Robert and I arrived late at RegalCare Manor, after dinner had been served. As we entered his wing, there was a smell of oldness, decay, enclosed air. TVs blared different stations at full blast, two in every room. The shared room he was assigned to was very shabby. Someone in marketing must be highly paid for the irony of the facility's name "RegalCare," I thought.

I felt like we were refugees: *Here is your spot. Here is your food.* I unpacked some of his things, set up the nightstand, tried to figure out the bed. Robert was quiet, "cooperative." A duo of aides came in to weigh him: 108 pounds. Another team, including the floor and head nurses, came in to examine him all over—teeth, skin, eyes, ears—creating their own benchmark of Robert's physical status. Flomax and Atavan had been prescribed. I told Robert I would come to see him tomorrow. I was trying unsuccessfully to be cheerful. On the way out I stopped at the nurses' station to introduce myself and tell them Robert and I were long-time friends, and I mentioned Marcy, so they would know he had some people looking out for him. I told them that Robert occasionally heard voices.

"You mean the dementia," the nurse said.

"Well, not exactly. He might be getting out of his bed tonight. He may need a different medication."

"Dementia," she repeated, and I got the hint that mental illness must be presented as dementia here. And what difference did it make, anyway? "We have the bed alarm on. We'll know if he gets out of bed."

When I came to the nursing home the second time Robert was dressed and tidy, his hair combed. It was a relief to see him "put together," a kind of antidote to everything else.

I had only been in a nursing home once or twice before. I felt humbled, trying to take in this whole strata of experience common to so many—families and friends and spouses and children and the souls who were in the facility themselves. And their aides, with their own stories—an endless 24-hour cycle of physical maintenance. And yet, awful as RegalCare Manor was, with the 40 or so patients on that wing in 40 different states of deterioration or, in a few cases, rehabilitation, it was a better situation than the apartment where Robert had been alone so long. I paid rent for a final month there and cleaned his apartment one Saturday. John and a friend came to unload the furniture that his neighbors didn't want. I vacuumed the floor, pointlessly. At a cost of $14,800 per month for the nursing home, Robert's money would be gone quickly. I completed the application for Medicaid.

On my second visit, Robert was amenable to going outside, but unsteady on his feet, so they found us a wheelchair and I pushed him all around the building. There was not much to see, just the sidewalk and the green woods surrounding the place, but it was a sweet sight compared to the neighborhood outside his apartment building in East Bridgeport. Robert was quiet, but it was not an angry quiet. How like a boy was his head from behind, the small delicate white-haired skull and large, almost eager, ears on each side. How he had always been a boy. That wise, slow-speaking, authoritative, professor-ish attitude was a persona he created long ago to keep everyone at bay, and it had worked well. Now he needed us desperately, but that persona was ever in the way.

"You said you were going to take me home," he said, suddenly.

"No. I never said that." I stopped the wheelchair in the middle of the sidewalk.

"You did."

"I did not. I cannot make a home for you, Robert. I have tried, but it's not possible."

"Well," he said, cold and calm, "We differ on that."

How many times over the past months had I pictured him living with us, in the sunporch, an aide coming each day to look after him, the state of the bathroom, the constancy of his presence... It was impossible. Who would be caring for him? Should I quit my job? Was that what he wanted, really, to be my everything, as I was his everything? In his imagination, he took care of me.

After that visit, the coldness began. The seal-down. On the next visit, there was no warmth in his eyes. To keep him clean, they had shaved his beard, and he looked strange again to me. He did not want to go out. "I'm not going out there again," he said, pointing to the window. "I have a very good friend," he said, now pointing to the hallway, where Doreen, the aide on this shift, was pushing a man in a wheelchair. "She takes care of me. All the time. Every day. I really mean it." He nodded to emphasize his point.

"I'm glad," I said. And I was. On my next visit his good friend was Colette, another aide. He needed a Good Friend, and I was no longer it. In his flat gaze I could see that he barely recognized me, and the recognition he did have was of someone who had done him wrong. I felt afraid of the mental illness embodied in my friend, all his loss and anger funneled through the persona and outward toward me, even though he didn't mean to direct it that way. I repeated to myself: *He doesn't mean to.*

Swaddled under two fleece blankets, he had just woken up and saw that I was there, standing in the dark room. His roommate Bill was asleep or pretending to sleep with an eye mask on and the curtain drawn between the beds. Bill's oxygen machine made a brief ping and hiss.

"Forget it," Robert said to me as though I had spoken. "Just forget it." His eyes were tired and cold. He looked away. "I have a bad heart." Pause. "They're very kind to me here." Pause. He turned his head to glare at me. "There isn't any money; there never was any money." He pulled the soft blanket closer under his chin and looked away. "I have a bad heart," he said again.

"I'm not Them!" I made my claim, pathetically. "I've been your friend for over 40 years. I brought you a cup of coffee." I made a move to come closer to the bed.

"No!" he yelled, waving me away.

"I brought communion," I said, softer. I had gotten the wafer at church the day before and it was carefully stashed in the pyx in my bag. "Do you want communion?" I asked, aware of the irritation in my voice. He looked away.

"I'm leaving then. Maybe it would be better if I don't visit."

He refused to look in my direction. "Yes."

Would it be better if I didn't visit? I could not explain to him anymore why he had to be here; he didn't want to hear it (physically he could hardly hear it anyway), and then he would forget. The aides and nurses liked him. "Everything I do, he says, 'God bless you, God bless you'," Jean-Michelle, the night nurse on C-Wing, said, smiling. Better that he treated me badly and them well, I thought. Better that he simply forget me, while I scrounged up his tax returns and divorce decrees for the Medicaid application, and distributed his duplicate hammers and screw drivers and work gloves to neighbors and friends.

He needed warm sweatpants, the aide told me; he was always cold. Instead of visiting, I shopped for sweats.

On the way home my prayer again was *Release him, release him*. But my real prayer was "Release me," and on that day it occurred to me that it probably would not be answered until I really wanted the release for him, not me.

Now that Robert refused to go outside, his delusions were more steady, trapped in the bed with him, the main difference being that there were many people to bring him food, clean him, check on him. He was friendlier with Marcy, who visited with her husband every Sunday and brought communion to him.

After he waved me away like one of his Bad People, I did not visit him for three weeks. I no longer felt guilty for putting him in the nursing home; my guilt came from the relief I felt at being dismissed, freed for a time from my anticipation of seeing him, and the sadness of what simply was. What stage was this? Depression, acceptance? It didn't matter.

It was a Wednesday evening when I came back to visit him again. When I checked in, Jean-Michelle shook her head, exasperated. "He cry out 'Help me!', then just yelling at us all to get away," she said.

"Well, good luck to me," I replied, with the now-familiar anxious anticipation of seeing him, unsure what state of mind he would be in. Would he see me or not?

I stood a moment while he dozed, looking at him. He did not leave the bed anymore, Jean-Michelle had said; they changed his diapers regularly. His cheeks were hollowed out; it appeared that he no longer felt cold or hot and slept in a gray T-shirt under the quilt. I sat down in the chair by the bed. His mouth needed wiping. A scoop of chocolate ice cream was melting in a Styrofoam cup on the tray table. Bill, his roommate, was not there.

How long could this go on? As long as it would go on. I refused to think about it. This dying was like labor, only more unpredictable in its ways and pains, without a child at the other end of suffering. *Giving birth to death*, I thought.

Then Robert opened his eyes and saw me, his face softening in recognition. He put his hand out and I clasped it. His grip was familiar, surprisingly strong. He was saying something. His words were slurred but I recognized them finally. "I love you," he said. "I love you. I love you." He repeated it several times looking intensely at me, as though in a hurry, stroking my arm. He seemed to like touching my arm and I was glad I was wearing a soft sweater.

"I love you, too, my friend," I said, starting to weep, finally.

Robert smiled and for a moment I could see him in his eyes—a look like he used to give me across the table, the gaze I couldn't bear but now welcomed. He looked away at something in the room that I could not see and waved his arm as if to push it away. Then he looked back at me.

"Everything will be alright," he said, clutching my hand. "I know it will be." His words seemed to soothe him.

"You are right, Robert. It will be. You don't need to worry." Something else needed saying, but I was not sure what it was.

"I've written it all down," I said, the statement which had now become a joke between us. "Thank you for encouraging me. All these years." My words seemed very formal.

He seemed to understand and half-smiled at me.

Two days later he died. Fr. Tom and Marcy had visited in the morning. He was having trouble breathing and they had to get the nursing staff to clear the mucous from his mouth. Robert clung to Marcy's hand while Fr. Tom gave him absolution.

After work I had come by again. Robert was awake and restless, pushing his blanket off, but he did not see or hear me, staring over my shoulder. Around 1 a.m. in the morning the nursing home called to tell me he had stopped breathing. John and I drove over. They had cleaned him up and lowered the bed. He looked peaceful enough, empty and light, as though he could blow away. He had his release. I did, too.

We gave Robert a good send-off at St. James with a memorial Mass two weeks later, with 40 to 50 friends who knew him through us and others from church. John and I shared the eulogy. Many people were surprised at how long we had known each other. Some had worked with him at the Parish Center and had adapted to Robert's eccentricities; others remembered him as a lector, the way he could read scripture in such a way that you knew you had really heard it. Afterward, we ate sandwiches and cookies and socialized in the Parish Center. Few others had known Robert, really, except Marcy and Fr. Tom, but that didn't matter. The gathering held all of us.

After he died, I found another copy—the third—of Kinnell's *The Book of Nightmares*. This was the one he had given me when I had just turned 17, a month into our friendship. I saw my pencil notations alongside words I had looked up, trying hard to figure it out, to be good, to like it, to be the writer he had already told me I was. But I had forgotten that Robert had inscribed the book, with lines broken like a poem:

> Virginia,
>
> This is a life of great care
> a book of considerable honesty
> of risk and courage
> an act of love.
>
> Someday create a better life
> a better book than this
>
> But if it should ever happen
> Sometime that you find yourself
> "emptied of all Wind Singing—of light"
> share this with someone.
>
> Together you'll discover its care
> and your own, for the book
> for each other

through another's trust
your own beauty
                                    Robert

He loved me. It was not an illusion.

"The Joy of a Day"

Can it ever be true—
all bodies, one body, one light
made of everyone's darkness together?

*"Dear Stranger Extant in Memory
on the Blue Juniata"*

O n the last beautiful weekend of October, I drove the
three hours to Williamstown to spend the day on my
own at the Clark Art Institute. I arrived before the museum
opened and hiked up the hill to the cow pasture where Robert
and I had visited twice before. There were the trees that had
grown together in a strange hybrid of birch and maple. There
was the spot in the field where I had taken a nap while Robert
wandered.

In my backpack I had a pair of scissors and the heavy plastic
bag with his ashes. For the past few weeks, not knowing what
to do with them, we had kept the blue velvet bag of Robert's
ashes on our kitchen table, next to where he used to sit. It
seemed appropriate somehow. The night before I had decided
somewhat spontaneously, with John's blessing, that this hill
would be a good place to scatter his ashes. Despite the early
hour, there were a few people around, taking in the view,
chatting with each other. I waited for them to move along

before I took out the bag. I cut off top of the bag, under the industrial plastic tie. I put my hand into the fine gray powder of him that was more like dust than ashes, soft and slightly sticky, and let him go, handful by handful, over the field, taking my time. There was a slight breeze, which caught the dust from my hand and carried it off, like mist. I felt like a sower, each fling a bit more exuberant. "You would like this," I said aloud to him. I imagined him laughing, thought of his note: "for the joy of a day." I tossed a handful onto the boulder which sat under a maple tree in the middle of the field. The bag was empty. I climbed onto the boulder and sat for a while. A cricket chirped. The orange leaves rustled overhead.

The fall sky was blue, deep blue, like something loyal and faithful. In a small hollow of the rock next to me I saw a tiny chip of bone and some dust of him. I had *The Book of Nightmares* in the backpack.

"I'll read you something, okay?" I said, and read him a part of that opening poem:

> "And in the days
> when you find yourself orphaned,
> emptied
> of all wind-singing, of light,
> the pieces of cursed bread on your tongue,
>
> may there come back to you
> a voice,
> spectral, calling you
> sister!
> from everything that dies.

And then
you shall open
this book, even if it is the book of nightmares."

His life had been a book of nightmares, much of it. I never wanted to see that. I always just wanted it to be different.

"Are you going to put me somewhere?" I thought of his repeated question over those many months, scrawled on that note when he felt truly desperate.

Yes, dear one, I put you somewhere. I had to. I hope you understand how we could not take care of you. I think you do, now.

So. Are you "one with all that is," as Fr. Tom would say? Will we "know each other" when it's my turn, not so very long from now, when things will be past "now" and "then," past imagination, and therefore past the words that were so precious to us?

Where is home? Who is home? Perhaps home is to be known, and so you were known, Robert, as best we could know you. Why did I write it all down? Because I always have. It was a way to know you, and me, and what separates us and what binds us. It's love, you know.

The story, our story, dear friend, is good.

Little sleep's-head sprouting in the moonlight,
when I come back
we will go out together,
we will walk out together among
the ten thousand things,
each scratched too late with such knowledge, the
    wages
of dying is love.

"*Little Sleep's-Head Sprouting in the Moonlight*"

Acknowledgements

This short book has been a *long* time in the making and I have been lucky to have some excellent friends and readers along the way—all of them also fine writers. My thanks to Lewis Buzbee, Dale Neal, Nat Whitten and Sam Ogles for their early readings; to Helen Fremont for her helpful suggestions on a later draft; to Bob Ayres for multiple patient readings and his faith in the story; to Florence Kraut for her keen questions and ongoing encouragement; to my sister Carolyn Weir for clarifying details and for being there; and to Barbara Mariconda for her fine editing skills, enthusiasm, and steady, life-giving friendship. And, of course, there's John…

I also wish to thank Rev. Thomas Lynch, Marcy Kelly, and the community of St. James Roman Catholic Church in Stratford, Conn., for their kindness and support of Robert—and me—during those years.

About the Author

Virginia Weir grew up in the Southwest, graduated from San Francisco State University, and completed an MFA in fiction from Warren Wilson College. Throughout a life of writing, she has worked as a typesetter, database administrator, grant writer, and fundraiser. She lives with her husband in Connecticut. www.VirginiaWeir.com

Made in the USA
Middletown, DE
29 December 2020